EXACTLY HOW TO SELL

Phil M Jones

EXACTLY HOW TO SELL

The Sales Guide for Non-Sales Professionals

WILEY

For general information about our other products and services, please contact our Customer Care Department within the United States at (800) 762-2974, outside the United States at (317) 572-3993 or fax (317) 572-4002.

Wiley publishes in a variety of print and electronic formats and by print-on-demand. Some material included with standard print versions of this book may not be included in e-books or in print-on-demand. If this book refers to media such as a CD or DVD that is not included in the version you purchased, you may download this material at http://booksupport.wiley.com. For more information about Wiley products, visit www.wiley.com.

Library of Congress Cataloging-in-Publication Data

Names: Jones, Phil M, 1981- author.
Title: Exactly how to sell : the sales guide for non-sales professionals /
    Phil M Jones.
Description: Hoboken : Wiley, 2018. | Includes index. |
Identifiers: LCCN 2017049914 (print) | LCCN 2017050805 (ebook) | ISBN
    9781119473466 (pdf) | ISBN 9781119473398 (epub) | ISBN 9781119473459
    (hardback)
Subjects: LCSH: Selling. | Marketing. | BISAC: BUSINESS & ECONOMICS / Sales &
    Selling. | BUSINESS & ECONOMICS / Marketing / Telemarketing.
Classification: LCC HF5438.25 (ebook) | LCC HF5438.25 .J6586 2018 (print) |
    DDC 658.85—dc23
LC record available at https://lccn.loc.gov/2017049914

Cover Design: Wiley

Printed in the United States of America
10 9 8 7 6 5 4 3 2 1

*To my friend Randy Richman, for giving me
more than he will ever get to know.*

CONTENTS

INTRODUCTION

This book is designed to do exactly what the title says: to provide you with a hand-held walk through the myriad factors that influence the decision-making process and allow you to achieve more success through empowering more people to choose you, your product, or your service.

Personally, I have been a student of self-development from as early as I can remember. I've attended countless seminars, read hundreds of books, and invested time to learn from an abundance of exceptional people. The reality was that from each of these prior studies, on every occasion, I failed to retain all the information and only managed to use the parts that where most relevant at that time.

When I decided to write this book, my goal was to provide something that would serve readers in many ways. You can read it cover to cover, scribbling notes and actions for yourself; you could lift parts of it and use them to train your own people; or you could keep it close by and use it for inspiration as you go through changes in your business and are looking for some external influence. Above all else, remember that this is your book—a working document. Scribble on it, place markers in it, and make it your own. It is expected to spark ideas and actions that are not written on these pages, so it may help to keep a notepad handy as you craft your own action list inspired by the lessons you absorb from this read.

Refining your craft as you grow your own success is an ongoing discovery and this book is something that can be revisited time and time again as you look to launch new ideas, are looking for flashes of inspiration or you are preparing for a new opportunity. Each time you read it then expect to take something new from it, this is a sign of your personal growth and the circumstances you are currently in. Take ownership of this book and use its guide to spark curiosity in you to further develop your skills in winning business by exploring the works of others as you take deeper dives into the principles shared with you.

Your next big break could be just one call or meeting away, let's see how what you learn in this read can get you better prepared to seize that moment.

EXACTLY HOW TO SELL

1

A SHIFT IN MIND-SET

It is rare that you meet a child who has aspirations of growing up to be a salesperson. You do hear alternatives such as politician, lawyer, doctor, sports professional, or artist—and in all these examples, the commonality is that without the ability to influence, persuade, and negotiate, the chances of success are highly reduced.

Having a talent or ability to perform is not enough by itself to secure success. Through the years there have been countless examples of highly capable businesspeople failing because of one simple reason: they did not know how to sell.

SALESPEOPLE OR SALES PROFESSIONALS

Finding yourself in a sales role quite often happens by accident. Perhaps you have just started in business or had an urgent business need, or maybe somebody else has put you into the role. The truth is we are all salespeople, and in every part of life, sales skills are useful tools in helping us to climb the ladder and realize more of our potential. When you reflect on almost everyone who has achieved a significant level of success, you will typically find that their achievement has been enabled, amplified, or accelerated through their ability to sell.

"Sales" is certainly not a dirty word. To illustrate my point, here are some high achievers I would class as being some of the most successful sales professionals on the planet:

- Steve Jobs
- Martha Stewart
- Leonardo DiCaprio
- Martin Luther King, Jr.
- Nelson Mandela
- Sir Alex Ferguson
- LeBron James
- Richard Branson
- Oprah Winfrey
- J. K. Rowling

There is probably a huge difference between your initial image of a salesperson and these decorated professionals.

During my seminars I often ask audience members to reach for adjectives that would describe a stereotypical salesperson. Common responses almost always include these words:

- Pushy
- Greedy
- A con man
- Obnoxious
- Overly friendly
- A liar
- Annoying

How would you feel if someone used those words to describe you? I would imagine less than happy. I also imagine that one of the reasons you picked up this book is your fear of being perceived that way.

In seminars, I then ask the same audience to reach for adjectives that do not describe a "stereotypical" salesperson, but a "professional" salesperson. The list of adjectives is quite a contrast:

- A good listener
- Problem-solving
- Empathetic
- Genuine
- Knowledgeable
- Helpful
- Responsible

I always find this experiment incredibly interesting. It becomes obvious to me that the fear of being a salesperson is the fear of being perceived as carrying that first set of attributes. Today's world is a very different one, and given our reality—the huge transparency now created through reviews, the Internet, and the power of a consumer's voice on social media—then it really only leaves room for the sales professional to prosper.

Choosing to be professional means you are faced with two options for acquiring new customers. One option is to be reactive, await your inquiries, and respond promptly on receipt of some interest, and the second is to be proactive and take steps to make things happen.

Although there are plenty of strategies that can result in you creating more inbound inquiries, it is paramount that you take control of your circumstances and build a robust plan to proactively reach more potential customers. Success in sales is all about maintaining control. By building a process that allows you to direct and steer your future customer numbers, you can build your business with far more control and composure. Relying purely on a reactive approach will bring huge variance, with external factors largely responsible for your success or failure.

CHOOSING YOUR FOCUS

A significant difference between marketing and sales is that marketers look to attract new customers, while sales professionals take the time to choose their customers. If you can look back over your experience and think of a customer you wish you hadn't had, then I imagine that was not somebody you strategically chose as a perfect customer.

Choosing your customers ahead of time is a process known as "prospecting." Outside of the world of sales, the word is defined on Wikipedia as "the first stage of the geological analysis ... of a territory. It is the physical search for minerals, fossils, precious metals or mineral specimens . . . . Prospecting is a small-scale form of mineral exploration which is an organized, large-scale effort undertaken by commercial mineral companies to find commercially viable ore deposits." This can be simply translated as the hunt for buried treasure. It's about extracting the maximum value from the relationships that we hold, the circumstances we find ourselves in, and the opportunities we create.

Your responsibility as a sales professional is to constantly be on the hunt for buried treasure. As a treasure hunter, you would have predetermined goals identifying the high-value items you are looking for. As a sales professional, your job is to do exactly the same thing: decide in advance the precise, perfect people you would love to do business with.

Striving for more and having ambition are qualities that have fueled the sales profession since the start of time. This enthusiasm can also be a huge barrier to you taking advantage of the opportunities that are already available. You have the right to choose your customers, decide what success looks like, and identify the quality and quantity of people that you would like to work with. A common mistake is that people fail to execute that choice and find themselves trying to work with anybody and everybody.

I choose to take the perspective that every future customer is no more than a "missing person." Instead of looking for anybody and everybody, get laser focused on exactly what your ideal customer looks like—to the point that you could describe them to a stranger, as you would with a missing person. Once you have that focused description in your mind, you will see opportunity more often, get more of the right kind of customers, and be more targeted in all of your activities. The additional benefit you gain once you can explain each of your target markets is that other people can help you to hit the target. You can describe them to everyone you meet and let those people introduce you to your missing people or opt in to be potential customers themselves.

There is a part of the brain called the reticular activating sensor (RAS) that is a component our conscious system. It makes decisions throughout the day as to what information is important and what we should ignore. Setting your RAS on the precise customer you would love to meet next means that you start to see and create opportunity everywhere you go. I am not saying that you will only deal with people who fit your perfect description, but simply being more targeted in your activity means you get lucky more often. I view it just like the game of darts. Every time you throw a dart, you are aiming for something specific. You don't always hit it, yet each time you miss, you still contribute to your score.

To identify your missing people, you can work through three simple steps:

1. Imagine your dream customer, the perfect person you would love to work with repeatedly. Once you are clear on this picture, take pen to paper and write a list of the exact qualities of this person and the reasons they are perfect for you.

2. In addition to the list of attributes, you may then need to apply some constraints and boundaries that narrow your gaze and place you in a stronger position to start identifying precise candidates:
   ○ Where are they located geographically?
   ○ What industry or sector are they in?
   ○ How big are they?
   ○ How long have they been doing what they do?
   ○ Who specifically within the company are you looking to help?
   ○ Why specifically would they need you?
   Combining the answers to these questions with the qualities from your list will put you in a very strong position to identify potential customers.

3. Create a detailed written profile of the precise people you are looking to do business with and make it as visually appealing as possible. This is your chance to create your "missing person" poster and share the details with all the stakeholders involved in your business.

If you have a range of products and services and have different target markets for each, then simply repeat the process for each specific audience.

Building Your Prospect List

If you are to proactively drive your success as a sales professional, then you must take control by creating a definitive list of potential customers who meet the predetermined criteria you have just set. It is unlikely that you will gain more new customers than you have prospects, and the finest sales professionals always have an abundance of new opportunities ahead of them. Therefore, an essential part of every sales process is to identify a list of potential customers and add to that list as often as possible.

My general rule is to build a list with at least 10 times more than the number of new customers you desire. Start by building the list before approaching the people, because without a quantity of quality, you can quickly hit a dead end. This can dramatically affect your momentum and confidence when you are building your pipeline.

To help you build a massive list, I have developed a simple system for creating a sequential process to maximize your existing network and reach, delivering you a never-ending supply of names. Build your list of potential customers by following the FRIENDS system:

> **Friends**—Start your list by considering all your friends in life and business. Go through your phone contacts, e-mail contacts, social network connections, and address books, considering all people who fit your target market or could help you get closer to it, and add them to your list.
>
> **Records**—As we go through our professional lives, we collect reams of information that is full of potential future value. Go through existing and previous customer and supplier records, contacts from previous employment, and libraries of business cards.

Industry—Consider every industry that you would like to work with or have worked with in the past, and then add relevant individuals and companies from the same or similar industries.

E-marketing—The web is a fantastic tool for building your list. Put a contact form on your website to collect phone numbers and e-mail addresses in exchange for something of value, and use search engines to identify existing buyers of your product or service.

Networking—Attend events, both formal and informal, to identify future customers for you and your business.

Directory—Use directories of groups and organizations within your sector to gain the names and contact details of prospects. Start with the directories of groups you are associated with so that you have a common interest to make contact over.

Same Name—Finally, review your entire list and consider anyone you can think of who shares the same first or last name as any of your existing prospects. You will be amazed at how many names you add by following this simple memory technique. *Please remember that people buy people—your list must be of names of people, not organizations!*

BECOMING DEVILISHLY PRODUCTIVE

So now you have this giant list of people. As much as this is helpful, it can also be remarkably overwhelming. To professionally prospect a massive list is close to impossible, but your productivity can be enhanced by defining your focus and narrowing your gaze toward specific groups of people.

If you are to find the treasure, have long-term success, and be in a position in which you have a continuous supply of new business opportunities, you will likely need to look for prospects who fit into different groups. Invest the time to identify three different types of prospects before choosing your focus. You can choose to label these categories in a way appropriate to your circumstances, but to help with the clarity of the example, let's stick to the analogy of hunting for treasure.

LEVEL 1—SILVER PROSPECTS These are the opportunities that should be your easy wins and should provide you with the short-term success you need to keep doing business. They possibly came to you through a direct inquiry, have an immediate need, and are transactional in their nature. It is unlikely that these people are going to be big spenders; however, they make decisions quickly, are not very price sensitive, and are an essential part of your sales success.

LEVEL 2—GOLD PROSPECTS These are people you have proactively selected as potential valuable core customers of your product or service. Perhaps they are already buying from somebody else and may be a little slow to make their decision, but they have the ability to deliver an ongoing, repeat spend to you.

LEVEL 3—PLATINUM PROSPECTS These premium prospects are your high-reaching dream opportunities—perhaps the perfect sale, the ideal account, or the elusive "big fish." This is an opportunity that, if you were to secure it, could make your year or even be life altering for you personally. They are unlikely to have you on their radar, already have an abundance of others trying to win the same opportunities, and are notoriously challenging to get in front of.

Having these three categories means that you can split your big list into smaller areas and, before taking action, choose what type of customers you are currently looking for more of. All this preparation can still leave you paralyzed and lacking the focus to determine where to point yourself. You may have hundreds of potential customers in each area, so that this abundance of opportunity stops you from moving forward.

Instead of working with everybody, your next smart step is to become what I call "devilishly productive." The reason I call it this is because it involves taking each of your three categories and selecting just six specific contacts to work on in each area. Six silver, six gold, and six platinum prospects (666) gives you a workable total of just 18 people.

The first six "good" prospects become your bread-and-butter sales—they decide quickly and drive instant profit and opportunity into your business. They're unlikely to make you whoop and holler with excitement, but these are the people you need to keep moving forward and help feed you on the journey to find the people who are going to close in your next six.

This next six people you focus on are your "better" prospects. These are the ones who, when you do secure them, make for a good day. This is when you get super excited, so this is your gold—what you're really looking for.

The last six people to work on are your absolute ideal prospects, those big fish, the ones who, if you land one, will make your life easier. Now, this might be an individual you want to join your business. It might be that dream transaction, where somebody buys everything you have to offer. Or it might be that perfect partner, the relationship that you know will manage to join those dots up and cause your business to skyrocket overnight.

Think about the differences between these three different groups of people. Those good prospects down at the first six should be easy to find and easy to close, and you should be able to work through them fairly quickly.

The second group of people might take a bit more time—time to find, time to get in front of and time to work through multiple meetings. It might take you a few weeks or months to get to a point where they make the decision you want them to make. But when they make it, you know it's worth it.

The final group are the slow burns. These are going to take the most time, effort, and energy. They're probably already working with somebody else. This isn't about getting them to choose you. The first decision you need to get these people to make is to choose to stop doing the thing you want to replace, so this will take time.

Choosing to become devilishly productive and working prospects in these three different areas means you're taking care of the day-to-day, you're looking at how you can be super successful, and you're also taking care of the dream ticket that we know is possible for you.

Staying focused on just 18 people means that as decisions are made, your list is always changing. As you close one successfully, enjoy the celebration, be proud of yourself and your achievement, but then immediately start thinking about who steps into their place the very next day.

The same goes when somebody decides they're not for you at this stage. When somebody says "No, not right now" to you, move them off your devilishly productive list, return them to your larger list, and bring somebody else into their place.

Being prepared to ask yourself every day "Who are the 18 prospects I'm working with at this moment?" is a very simple way to keep part of your activity focused on the continuous growth of your customer base.

SALES IS A PHILOSOPHY

In every business I have been a part of, there has typically been a clear divide between the sales and operational sides of the organization. Most people believe that the responsibility of winning and maintaining business is simply that of the sales team. I do not just disagree with this approach but believe it to be the failing of many businesses year after year.

If you are building a business that looks to connect with its customers, offer fantastic levels of service, and gain referrals and stacks of repeat business, then understanding that sales is a philosophy can help you get there.

When working with clients, it is essential for us to oversee the entire customer experience—from first contact, through the sales process, to delivery of the promise and beyond. The whole team has a significant impact on the commercial success of the company, and at every point of contact we have the chance to either enhance or reduce the quality of the customer experience. Getting this right brings such significant results, it's astounding. Bringing a commercially focused sales mind-set to every customer interaction can amplify your sales success in abundance. Having everybody pulling together in one direction creates benefits that are slight when looked at in isolation, yet the collective benefit is compounded to a result that will astound you. Shift your mind-set to your own process and ask yourself the following questions:

- How does the first point of contact with a customer support your sales outcome?

- How well does your operational team deliver on the promises made by the sales team?
- What specifically do you say in the sales process to set fair expectations for the process that follows?
- Are the sales opportunities being maximized at the point of delivery?
- What further information could be collected at each contact point that would support future sales success?
- Is the language and terminology used to describe your products and services consistent across all areas?
- Is your finance department aware of the potential value of each of your existing customers?
- Are relationships being layered within existing customers to protect loyalty, strengthen relationships, and increase the efficiency of transactions?

Connecting the dots in the process has several very tangible benefits, including

- Increases in profits
- No late payments
- No bad debts
- Preferential treatment from suppliers
- Increased operational efficiency
- Improved staff productivity
- More free time
- Reduced customer complaints
- Improved communication

Just imagine the positive impact on your sales success if you first choose to map your customer journey, identify the key checkpoints within it, and equip yourself and all key stakeholders with the correct skills and information to maximize each opportunity.

PERCEPTION IS REALITY

Unfortunately, in life and business, first impressions count. Humans are notoriously shallow and make judgments on others in the shortest periods of time and with very limited information. When you're asking others to part with money, these judgments can be even sharper, and the difference between someone choosing you and someone like you can be the slightest of factors.

Knowing that you are going to be facing huge judgment from potential customers, consider how you wish to be judged and take control over what others go on to think. However harsh a judgment may be, take confidence from the fact that creating this first impression is within your full control. The position you hold in your business, your personal experience, and the size and credibility of your organization are all unknown factors when you present yourself for the first time. This impression is your opportunity to set the bar at a place that you decide.

Your personal presentation is paramount. Your choice of outfit, fragrance, personal grooming, and accessories all say something about you. Are you happy with the message you are giving?

I am sure you can think of countless scenarios in which you have been prejudged or you have prejudged others. It is important to accept that this happens, but equally important to never prejudge others.

Some of the key factors that affect the immediate judgment others make of you are as follows:

Mode of transport—People's social standing is often judged by the car that they drive. Knowing this, please do all you can to use it as a tool. If your business requires you to be perceived as highly successful and your car echoes this, then make sure you get seen driving it. If your vehicle hasn't yet reached your business aspirations, then choose an alternative means of transport or ensure that it does not hinder your chances of success. This can also work the other way. If your business has a high-value offering and your car seems too expensive, then you too will be perceived as expensive and you may lose the work. What is imperative is that, whatever your means of transport, it is always presented at its best and is working for you, not against you.

Your uniform—Clothing is a tough one to get right. Many of us undertake a variety of roles in business and have a varied work life. My general rule is to dress as your customer would expect to see you, and if in doubt, you are better to be dressed more formally than too casual.

Your accessories—Accessories are often the most telling guide to someone's true personality. You can tell far more about people from their choice of shoes, jewelry, body art, business stationery, electronic devices, and luggage than from many other factors. Please take a moment to consider what yours say about you and whether they give the impression you are planning for.

Your grooming—Be prepared for people to judge you by what you look like, what you smell like, and how you behave. Ask a stranger to profile you based on your look and listen to the response. I learned an important lesson on an extended business trip when I looked down at my hands to see overgrown fingernails not representing me the way that I would choose. I mean, how can I take care of someone's business success if I cannot care for my own personal grooming? The entire meeting I kept my hands out of sight, lacked my usual confidence, and felt paranoid about my personal appearance. From that day onward, the manicure routine has taken high priority in my personal planning, and travel-sized nail clippers are a permanent fixture in my work bag! Please also consider your handshake: too firm and people will think you're arrogant; too weak and they will think you're incompetent.

Your marketing materials—Your business gives an impression, too. Whether it is your business card, your e-mail signature, your telephone voicemail, or your website that your prospects first bump into, be certain it is giving the right message. I work on the principle of presenting your business as the one you plan to grow into, not the one you are today. The quality of printing on your media gives an impression of the care and attention you take with your business. Giving a consistent message through all e-mail communication demonstrates structure and control. I recommend that all e-mail communication follows the same format, with fonts, spacing, and auto-signatures all being consistent. Your voicemail sets the tone and culture of your business. Your website should clearly explain how you help people and should reinforce your vision.

Understanding each component that contributes to the equation of your suitability for the job is one further area that you can control ahead of a sales opportunity. It also helps you think like a sales professional.

IS IT WORTH IT?

I learned early on that there is a big difference between doing the job right and doing the right job. I have always been hardworking and dedicated and put effort into every activity, striving toward the best results. The changing point came when I realized that just working hard and being good at what I did resulted in only limited success. The big lesson was that I needed to understand what my high-payoff activities really were.

We all have "stuff" that we need to do in our daily routines, but how much of that "stuff" really helps toward achieving the end result we are looking for? Run this simple equation for yourself and you will start to be able to make more informed decisions about where you choose to spend your time.

You will need to know the answers to the following questions:

A: How much money do you wish to earn in the next 12 months?

B: How many hours a week do you personally plan to work?

C: How many weeks of the year do you see yourself working?

Then calculate the following mathematical equation:

$$A \div B \div C = \text{Your hourly rate}$$

Only by knowing this number can you really start to look at your productivity and identify which of your activities are building your business and which are detracting from it. Anything you find yourself acting on that you would not pay yourself your desired hourly rate to do needs to be considered and questioned. Many of the activities you may have to learn to delegate, and some you may just stop doing completely.

The exercise typically results in people realizing that the following are the two most profitable activities:

1. Direct conversations with potential customers
2. Delivering goods or services for actual customers
     The reason they discover this is because of their knowledge of one more high-payoff activity:
3. Planning and review

The more of your time you invest in these areas, the more chances you create to grow your business.

THE VALUE OF A CUSTOMER

A common mistake that many people make is that they fail to see past the first transaction with a customer, and they measure their success or value based on the size of the initial piece of business.

Consider, for example, that you are in the business of cutting hair. Looking at the value of customers, you learn the average one spends $75. It would be easy to plan your business accordingly. If, however, you look at the bigger picture, you can soon start to identify the true value of this exact same customer.

EXAMPLE 1

Customer spends $75 a visit
Visits every 8 to 12 weeks
Remains a customer for 5 years
Taking into account the extremities of this example, the value of this customer is calculated as follows:

$75 × 4 visits per year × 5 years = $1,500 in lifetime value

EXAMPLE 2

Customer spends $95 a visit
Visits every 6 to 8 weeks
Remains a customer for 7 years
Introduces two new similar clients annually

Taking this more optimistic view helps us see a different potential value in a customer, calculated as follows:

$$\$95 \times 8 \text{ visits per year} \times 7 \text{ years} = \$5,320$$

plus a further 14 new customers who, if they do the exact same thing, result in a further $74,480 in revenue from a single relationship.

What I do know is that it is very rare you will get more money than you ask for or achieve greater success than you prepare for. If you see your customers as being worth $75, that is likely where you will set the bar. If you see your customers as being worth $5,320, then you will build an experience that is fitting for that. If you see their value as over $80,000, then you will do what it takes to prepare for that greater opportunity. Long-term success starts with taking a long-term view and preparing yourself by understanding the accurate potential lifetime value of your customers.

MAKE IT WORK ON PAPER

"If at first it does not work on paper, then how can we expect it to work in reality?"

This was a piece of advice I received early on in my career, and since then I have continually taken an analytical approach to growing businesses.

Every successful sale is the result of a combination of variables that lead up to that success. Imagine your sales process as a machine and every stage as a component in that machine. Typically, if a machine is not working as it should, it is rarely the whole machine that is at fault. It is simply that one or more of the components is not running efficiently. By monitoring and measuring, we can find the individual areas that require improvement and continually work to improve the end result. In big business, we call these data points key performance indicators (KPIs), and we use them to create a dashboard to monitor the factors that contribute to sales success.

To provide yourself with a valuable tool to keep track of the factors that influence your overall success, it is advisable to have at least five KPIs and no more than twelve.

Examples of areas to consider monitoring are as follows:

- Total number of sales opportunities per week, month, or year
- Outbound calls made
- Percent of sales versus target, budget, or previous year
- Minutes spent in sales conversations
- Time between inquiry and decision
- Marketing activity/lead creation
- Lead/appointment
- Appointment/sales conversion
- Average transaction value
- Number of transactions per annum
- Percent of additional sales items
- Pipeline value

As you repeat activities, you soon have the ability to create ratios. Once those ratios appear, you have the ability to measure the effectiveness of your actions. Only once you start measuring something can you really start to improve it.

THE TWO MOST IMPORTANT QUESTIONS

Before you rush into action communicating with potential future customers, there are two very simple and hugely profound questions that it's essential you know the answers to:

1. Who do you serve?
2. What problems do you solve for them?

Without detailed answers to these two questions, you will find yourself flailing in the sales process, lacking direction in your activity, and lacking conviction in your conversation. The clearer you are on your answers, the more prolific you will be in finding and converting customers. Successful selling starts with understanding your role in finding the right solution for the right person at the right time. Gone are the days of embellishing the attributes of a product or service and hoping the masses come running—start by aligning yourself with the right groups of people, finding clarity regarding the service you provide and the value it brings to the customer, and having confidence in delivering that value.

2

THE QUEST FOR CONFIDENCE

For you to have picked up this book and got this far, my guess is that you never set out to work in sales, but through an alternative skill, passion, or opportunity you have found yourself with the need to become more skilled in the area of salesmanship to support your core profession.

Perhaps the most important attribute to demonstrate in the world of sales is that of confidence, yet when your experience is low in this area, you can easily find yourself ill equipped for the task at hand. If you've never done something before, how can you expect to be confident in it? Knowing how important confidence is and knowing that it's an essential part of success, throughout my career I've studied exactly how confidence is created.

To find confidence in something, you need to move through three steps in your experience that are associated with that very thing:

1. **Knowledge.** The first thing you need to become more confident is a base level of understanding or knowledge about the thing in question.

   Let's take, as an example, a trivial task. Being British-born, I will use the example of making a cup of tea. The first thing you would need to do is to gain knowledge of the components that go into tea making, the techniques associated with it, and the different methods of producing the finished cups. You could watch videos, read manuals, and observe others to grow your knowledge of the art form and learn various methods. This step is essential, yet it will only take you so far.

   In a business context, I have met hundreds of trainers, lecturers, and other business professionals who can talk with deep knowledge about what is involved in achieving success, yet without the following steps, their value is limited.

2. **Experience.** Having started by gaining the theory, you are now able to move to the next step in your quest for confidence, which is gaining a feeling of confidence in yourself. The only way you can obtain a true feeling of confidence is following personal experience. It is only after having done something once that you will feel more capable of doing the same or better the next time—it creates a benchmark. Sticking with the example of making this cup of tea, this would mean taking everything you have learned, going through the process of pouring hot water over tea leaves in your chosen method, and learning from the results. Try it to get a feel for it, to get an understanding of the different results that can be

achieved, and try without the worry of making something perfect. Very quickly you learned that you can make it in a pot or a cup. You learned that what you need to do is pour hot water over a tea bag. You learned that it needs to steep for a while, but you're never going to understand the difference in taste until you've experimented a little, until you've tried the thing.

The only way to grow your confidence in the selling process is to gain the experience of being in hundreds of sales conversations. You must experience the easy ones, the challenging ones, the times you make big mistakes, and the subtleties that can create dramatic differences in direction. Be brave enough to start by gaining the experience. Forget about being perfect, and focus on what the experience teaches you.

3. Expertise. Only at this point can you start to develop your expertise. Expertise is the combination of knowledge and experience and results in your certainty in what you know. Having made almost as many cups of tea in my lifetime as I have experienced sales conversations, I have the ability to understand the difference between good and bad, I can appreciate the factors that create those differences, and I can be honest about the changes I would need to make to improve the next time.

    Creating this honesty about your own performance is what delivers the pivotal point for your self-confidence. Accepting what went well and what could be improved and having some knowledge about how you can make those improvements leads to a high-achieving mindset.

    You can learn a lot from the experience of others—gain knowledge from people who have walked the path before you. There are countless resources in this world to help you grow. Just be sure to understand that your fastest and most rewarding growth comes from taking what you have learned, putting it into practice, learning from the experience, and then being honest enough to get better for the next time.

This chapter explores tools and techniques that you can use to increase your confidence ahead of your sales conversations and give yourself a fair advantage by preparing properly in advance.

HAVE YOU DONE YOUR HOMEWORK?

It can be very easy to get lost in the details associated with your products or services and your profession as a whole. Please never lose sight of what industry you are really in—the one commonality for you and every other business in the land is that you are in the business of helping people. When you are looking to communicate with someone for the first time, ask yourself the following question: *Am I looking to fix the problem or help the person?*

I know what answer you are likely to give. I also know that most frequently, when people prepare for a sales conversation, the sole focus of that conversation is directed at fixing the problem, through embellishing on the brilliance of the product or service and explaining the detailed benefits that can help fix the problem.

It is unlikely that you will ever create a powerful enough connection with someone if your focus is aimed at solving the problem before you have gained their trust. Decisions are typically based on emotion, before any logic is involved in confirming them. You have a responsibility as a professional to know who it is that you are speaking with. A detailed knowledge of the customers you would like to have, the prospects you are working on, and your existing customers is a necessity in maximizing your success. The important thing to remember, though, is that people buy from people, not organizations. By researching and understanding what is important to the key decision makers you are approaching, you can cause your confidence to soar and your ability to create a connection and control a meaningful conversation to significantly increase.

Things that you should know ahead of a conversation are as follows:

- **What the prospect looks like**—Having seen a picture of your prospect ahead of time, you can instantly recognize them, and your greeting is likely to be warmer and more confident as a result.
- **Their hobbies and interests**—A knowledge of the person under the surface can help you identify factors that allow you to find common ground quickly.
- **The decision-making process**—Finding the names and positions of all others involved in the decision-making process gives you the ability to understand how far you can take each conversation and who else needs to be involved in the process.
- **Career history**—Knowing their length of service in the existing role, the companies they have worked with previously, and other industries they have served gives you numerous opportunities to steer a conversation to a position of confidence for all parties.
- **Mutual acquaintances**—Knowing who they know that you know gives you the chance to use those names in conversation and win trust from trading on existing trusted relationships.
- **Their competition**—In a B2B setting, an awareness of who they are looking to win business against quickly identifies you as being on their team, as an ally in helping them to achieve their goals.

- **Any public records or press releases**—Knowing their plans, awards, and recognition or any public acknowledgement of their contribution to the world gives you an inside track to be able to talk about their interests and objectives.

This can sound like a huge amount of work ahead of time, yet experience tells me that it saves a lot of time in the long run and positions you as a true professional when you arrive in the moment of the conversation. Much of the information is readily available should you choose to look for it. Years ago this would have been a huge task, yet today the Internet delivers for us almost instantly and typically without financial expense. Company websites give facts, and personal profiles such as those on Facebook, LinkedIn, and Twitter often provide a wealth of valuable information.

In a sales conversation you are looking to win the buyer's confidence that you are the right person for the job. It is very similar to an interview process for employment, and it is common knowledge that a candidate highly enhances their chances of success if they research the opportunity ahead of the interview. Increase your chances of winning the sale by doing your research ahead of time.

MAKING YOUR OWN LUCK

For many people looking to open a new door, a referred opportunity from an existing client or contact would be their ideal first approach. A referral provides a warmer opportunity, and because your chances of success are significantly higher, your confidence is high. This success is largely created through the transfer of trust between the source of the referral and the potential new buyer of your product or service.

By doing your homework, you can replicate this trust relationship with stone-cold prospects. Follow these three simple steps:

1. Find out who the potential buyer already does business with.

2. Find out who their fiercest competitor is.

3. Find out if you have a mutual acquaintance who is well respected, either a local or a national figure.

Once armed with this information, ensure your meeting includes the following three ingredients, in this order:

1. Start with an open discussion about how you both know, or have an interest in, the mutual acquaintance.

2. During conversation, mention the businesses that you work with that are the same as, or similar to, the organizations your prospect works with. If there are no familiar businesses, then name-drop your most recognized contact.

3. Toward the end of the meeting, subtly allude to a future conversation or interaction with their competitor.

Following these simple steps, what you achieve is instant rapport and trust thanks to the mutual acquaintance, then credibility from your awareness of others in their field. You then trigger a fear of loss from the mention of you possibly working with their competitor. Channeling these three steps through a sales meeting helps increase your chances of the buyer choosing to work with you.

TOOLS OF THE TRADE

Attending a sales meeting can be a daunting experience that often results in people either being massively underprepared or hiding behind their marketing literature. In every sales role I have been in, there are some essential "must haves" that are necessary for success. Everything else is just "nice to have" or, worse still, can stop you selling.

Notepad and pen—Taking notes before, during, and after meetings is a valuable task. It can ensure that you cover all you wish to cover, show that you are serious about doing business, help you listen effectively, and ensure that all relevant agreements are actioned. Don't leave home without them.

Watch—Time is an incredibly valuable resource to both sales professionals and customers. Ensuring you respect it is paramount in your success. Wearing a watch is a visual indicator that you value time.

Diary—Without a diary, you can't plan follow-ups, reschedule appointments, or prioritize actions. Today the concept of a diary spans from the traditional paper based to the more common electronic options that can be connected across multiple devices – The objective is to have access to your schedule at all times and can reference it in conversations with customers and prospects. Have it with you at all times.

Phone—The world of sales is fast paced and full of changing circumstances. The ability to communicate immediately is a necessity, and being able to pick up the telephone, have a real conversation, and make decisions helps you keep momentum. The phone is a sales professional's best friend.

Accurate client records—From the beginning of your journey, you should keep accurate records on all of your existing and potential customers. Whether it is computer-based CRM or a paper-based set of client files, maintaining a fluid record of communications and information will win you masses of extra business from having the perfect memory you know you don't have personally.

Data collection tool—Historically, people would hand out business cards and hope that it started the conversations desired. Instead, be ready to collect the contact details of others and land your permission-based introduction to them the minute you meet in person. Be ready to exchange numbers, swap e-mail addresses, or connect on a social media platform—just decide how you do it and be ready to move quickly when the moment arises.

Order forms—It may seem obvious, but the number of times I have seen sales staff miss opportunities because they did not have the ability to take an order there and then …!

Many of you reading this are perhaps thinking that there are tons of other items essential in your business, and perhaps you are right.

However, please consider that the salesperson's job is to give the prospect enough information to make a decision and then to ask for that decision. Very often, pre-prescribed sales presenters, product catalogues, and samples can all give customers the feeling of being sold to and gain a response of indecision, such as "Leave me a brochure and I will get back to you."

KEEPING YOUR HEAD IN THE GAME

Being responsible for winning new sales is tough. It comes with a list of challenges and obstacles that many of us never even knew existed before we started meeting with prospects and looking to influence decisions. It's certainly no easy ride; from the long days to the unpredictable outcomes, it can become difficult to maintain a positive outlook, optimistic attitude, and high energy level when the challenge of always looking for more is ever present.

There is no secret formula for overcoming these challenges, but over the years I have learned some simple skills and techniques that have really helped me and many of my clients to work through challenges and continue to build a successful book of business.

- Take the time to establish *why* you are doing what you are doing. Your business should be your vehicle to help you achieve all that you wish for in life. Write a detailed list of all the things that you wish to have, all the events you wish to experience, and all the qualities you wish to possess. In understanding your reasons for putting in all this effort, you will find the determination that will help you plow through those challenging times.

- Consider who you take advice from. You are being conditioned by your environment from the very first moment you are born, and those who you spend your time with have a massive impact on your life. I have had countless lessons of this where I have experienced both extremes, from very positive to very negative conditioning. However, the people we need to consider most are those who are closest to us. Our loved ones, families, and friends all have significant feelings, and they often reveal their duty of care and safety when they add doubt and caution to your plans. As a result of this, I very rarely speak about business with my family, since they have been conditioned by a very different world. Take the advice you need to grow your business exclusively from those who have achieved what you are looking to achieve.

- Visualize your achievements. Most people have a giant list of uncompleted tasks on some variation of a to-do list. Trying to complete the impossible task of clearing that list can be tiresome at best, and it certainly has a negative effect on your confidence when you are looking at a mountain of incomplete actions. Your confidence is created from your experience. I am certain that across your life to date you have catalogued hundreds of meaningful achievements and forgotten the fact that you have a proven track record of success. Counteract your list of incomplete tasks by running a record of achievement and documenting as many of your personal successes as possible. Go back as far as you can remember, list your victories, and keep adding to the list. Maintaining a victory journal like this, as well as surrounding myself with any awards, trophies, and photos of proud moments, keeps my self-doubt at bay by reminding me that I'm building on past successes.

- Have a mentor. Choosing someone that can bring you their experience, help answer questions, and ask you the questions you are too afraid to ask yourself is a great aid when dealing with challenging times. Remember that it is your job to choose the mentor, rather than them choosing you.

- Win when you are winning. It is very easy to take your foot off the gas and enjoy the limelight when you reach a level of success. Be your own champion, and when things are going well for you, keep riding that wave and enjoy the momentum it goes on to create.

KNOW YOUR ENEMY

The existence of competitors in your space confirms that you have a true market and provides you with benchmarks to be compared against. Nobody wants to win a one-horse race. Understanding the position you play within your entire marketplace is essential for you to be able to sell yourself and your offering appropriately.

Take the time to explore how you are similar to your competition and identify the exact things you do that are different. You may find the nuances of your difference in the "why" or the "how" you do things, more so than the specifics around "what" you do.

It is highly likely that you will find yourself in many conversations in which you are selling against a competitor. To appear different from your competitors, you must demonstrate that you are different and act differently. It is only possible to enhance your position of difference if you know what you are being compared to. Conduct an analysis of each of your competitors and find out exactly how you can outmaneuver them, grow your market share, and intelligently talk about the value of your offering in comparison to theirs.

The minimum areas for you to analyze are the components of a SWOT analysis. Bring your awareness to these areas:

Strengths—In which specific areas do you feel your competitor has an advantage over you?

Weaknesses—In what areas is your competitor currently exposed?

Opportunities—How can you position your offering to create an advantage for yourself?

Threats—Where do you need to protect yourself from the strength in their offering, and how could this affect your success?

The knowledge you gain from this is only to be used to position your value within the marketplace. To be respected by your customers, never devalue yourself by down-talking your competitors. Simply talk about what they do and what you do differently.

LEVELS OF SUCCESS: THINKING BIG

A phrase that has echoed around sales seminars for decades is that every "no" is just one step closer to a "yes." Although I understand that the premise behind this statement is persistence, optimism, and determination, I have always struggled with its practicality in the real world.

The truth, through my personal experience, is that every time I hear the word no, it hurts. We take this rejection personally, and this underlying fear of rejection is one factor that prevents many very talented people from realizing what they are truly capable of.

Placing such strong emphasis on the concrete outcome of the sales discussion encourages two very negative outcomes. The first is this immense pressure applied to gain the sale in the moment, and the second is the belief that the amount of success available is contained and finite. The result can then be that you find yourself holding back on opportunities for fear of rejection, or, perhaps more typically, finding yourself celebrating success before the job is complete.

Think about every transaction you have ever been a part of. When you think of each one honestly, you will realize that there was always more opportunity available and more that you could have mined from the moment. Your enthusiasm, combined with your lack of preparation, can result in you leaving the conversation and later thinking of what you should have said, the questions you could have asked, or the tools that would have supported your success.

The solution for this is to plan your multiple levels of success before every opportunity and consider the specific outcomes you plan to achieve ahead of time. You have complete control to decide the components of your own success in every conversation. The following nine steps make up a typical premeeting plan for me and my clients:

1. Give a good representation of myself and my company.
2. Build rapport.

3. Create a genuine opportunity to introduce our services.
4. Give the buyer enough information to make an informed decision.
5. Gain a decision.
6. Discover what future opportunities may arise.
7. Schedule our next action.
8. Ask for referrals.
9. Gain a referral.

Considering all these desired outcomes ahead of time allows you to become masterfully prepared and develop a conversation track for your discussion, and it significantly reduces the chances of you forgetting to bring something, say something, or do something in the moment. It is great practice to physically document your desired outcomes for every sales conversation ahead of time, and there are a number of very tangible reasons why.

CONFIDENCE

Success in sales is not black and white. Very often customers do not make up their minds to do business with us in the first meeting. By understanding which level of success you have achieved with your buyer, you have removed the yes/no outcome from the agenda, and you never actually fail. The worst that you have to deal with is that you have just not succeeded *yet*!

Making the first level of success something within your control provides you with the ability to always succeed to a point. Providing that you continually hit this one, the ball is in play and you have already started to succeed. The trick is to understand that no two scenarios are the same, and sometimes you will race up these steps in one meeting, whereas on other occasions it will take a long time.

However, at each point you are winning, and confidence is best achieved through compounding previous successes. Breaking success into smaller levels creates far more opportunities to feel like you are winning. Success regularly breeds more success.

STRUCTURE

Planning out your success before you have started can keep you in control and give you direction. It allows you to go through each level one at a time and tick them off in your mind. If you imagine it as building some flat-packed furniture, you are far more likely to achieve the finished piece by working through the instructions one step at a time and in the right order, as opposed to opening all the boxes and hoping for the best.

You have the ability to write your own structured and systematic process ahead of every major conversation. Through planning, doing, and repeating, you will find yourself having more and more control over the conversations you are a part of.

GETTING MORE

Instead of closing the meeting after the first decision, you now have the ability to add more to your agenda, gather additional sales, learn more information, and collect other valuable resources. Steering the next steps keeps you firmly in the driver's seat and results in increased immediate sales and future opportunities. It also saves you time in follow-up.

3

OPPORTUNITY IS
EVERYWHERE

The first two chapters have been invested in preparing you to
become more successful in your conversations. The art form
of selling is heavily geared toward your ability to create opportunities and influence the decisions of others to part with money and
get the goods or services you supply.

Earlier you learned that to commercially succeed in sales, you
must know the answer to two very powerful questions:

1. Who are the people that you serve?
2. What are the problems that you solve for them?

The more you gain clarity over your answers to these questions,
the more you'll realize that the profession of selling is not only
essential but also remarkably helpful to the entire community.
People can be notoriously indecisive, procrastinate repeatedly, and
fail to achieve their own goals and wishes because of not knowing

what action to take. In your profession, you hold a responsibility to look out for the people who need your help, be ready to win their trust, and help guide them through the decision-making process, so that you help those who can benefit from what you do to go on and actually realize that benefit.

Decide today that you are on a mission to help people and that the role you play as a sales professional is in service to those people. Quickly you will start to see that the opportunity to help is everywhere and the potential for you to grow your customer base is abundant.

This chapter explores precise techniques and skills to capitalize on the amount of opportunity that does exist and to lead you to more opportunities to sell.

WHAT FACE ARE YOU WEARING?

Building rapport is a crucial skill when you are looking to attract new customers, and it starts with one simple action that is often overlooked. The first thought someone has when they meet you for the first time is "Do I find you attractive?" We are all proven to be more attractive when we are smiling.

The wondrous thing about a smile is that it is infectious. If you smile at someone, they can't help but smile back! Think back to the times in the past when you were dating or, dare I say it, flirting. It all starts with a smile. Smiling is the best ice-breaker you have to start a new relationship, and its importance is often overlooked. Your smile is far more than just lifting the corners of your mouth and showing your pearly whites. Transferring the warm energy of a smile affects many more areas.

- **Facial expressions**—Smiling is something that we do with our whole face. We have all seen a child's face on the morning of their birthday—this is an example of a complete smile. How often are you wearing yours?
- **Body language**—Understanding that you smile with your whole body is a key lesson when attracting people to you. Open body language and a positive stance attract people. Check how you carry yourself in public and ensure you are open for conversation.
- **Voice**—Anyone who sells or has bought over the telephone knows that you can hear a smile. In the first few seconds of a call you can hear the warmth in the voice, which affects your instant decision about whether you like or dislike the person. Be in the zone before ever picking up the phone.
- **Company image**—Consider the "smile" your whole company makes. From your logo to your dress code to the way you answer your phones—all demonstrate your company's personality, and all can help to attract new customers.

You probably think that you are a pretty happy person most of the time, but sometimes it can be too easy to forget to tell your face! As creatures of habit, we need reminders. Reminders to turn on your "happy face" when you are in the marketplace can be the nudge you need to smile more. Place memory joggers in your environment that act as a switch to trigger your happy face. Over the years, I have introduced mirrors on the doors of retailers' staff areas with sayings like "Smile—you are on stage" attached to them, placed yellow happy-face emojis on the handsets of telephones in call centers, updated screensavers for office workers and created affirmations for the sun visors of traveling sales reps' cars—all with the purpose of creating a physical reminder that it's time to put your game face on.

NETWORKING FOR SUCCESS

As a professional, no matter your area of expertise, it is likely that at some stage you will find yourself within the mysterious world of business networking. Rooms full of new people, forced activities, business cards being tossed around like confetti, and an expectation of needing to see a return from your investment in time spent there can result in the entire experience being remarkably daunting.

Whether it is a formal, structured event or a large opening networking session, you are aware that within the room there is potential for new business and success could be just a conversation away. Why, then, can this exercise still strike so much fear into the attendees?

The reason you may find it difficult is because you were possibly conditioned as a child through a simple sequence of words: "Don't talk to strangers!" The first challenge is to defy that conditioning, and I've found that the easiest way to resolve this is to decide that pretty much everybody else is feeling the same as you. The belief that everyone is sharing a similar thought can reduce the anxiety a little, allowing you to relax enough to get involved.

Getting over the initial fear is one thing, however. To succeed in a network, here are some simple rules that have worked for me. I am sure if you choose to employ them, they could have significant benefits for you too.

- Have a plan. Regardless of the size of the event, it is unlikely that you can develop lasting business relationships with everyone in the room. No doubt there will be some people who will be of considerably more value to you than others. Set a goal and stick to it. It may be to make a number of new connections or to set a meeting with a specific person. Just turning up to see what happens is leaving your success to chance. If you can connect with people ahead of the event on a social network, then you can use the event itself for a formal meeting. If attendee lists are available ahead of time, then do research before the event and identify where you can best direct your efforts. A networking event is a highly leveraged opportunity to make new connections. Setting a plan ahead of time helps you maximize your time in the moment.

- Know what you are going to talk about. Starting a conversation is the hardest thing to do when entering a room full of strangers. To open conversation, the easiest place to start is by talking about a subject that you all have in common. The one subject that you all have in common is the event you are at. As such, plan a series of questions related to the event that allow you to be able to create a comfortable exchange and break the ice with strangers.

- Talk of how you help people. "So what do you do, then?" is a question that you are almost guaranteed to be asked, yet it often leaves the recipient flummoxed or flailing in their answer. Results can then include people sharing their company name or job title or the industry in which they work, and it very rarely results in an impactful follow-up conversation. Your goal from this question is to open up the conversation by being interesting to them. So when you are asked this question, please rephrase it in your head as "How do you help people?" and answer that question instead. A simple framework for your response could be "I help x achieve y." This allows the other person to ask more about what you do. Be prepared to share examples and stories of your work as opposed to facts.

- Sell to the room. This goes against what many experts train for networking, yet it is based on the simple reality that your best referrals come from existing customers. Therefore, to gain a quantity of referrals, you need a good number of people who have experienced working with you within your network. Now, this does not mean forcing your products or services on people; instead, look for ways that you can help those within your network with your expertise. Could you create an entry-level offering that makes it easy for people to experience what you do, or perhaps offer a complimentary audit, checklist, or review that shows people more of the value that you deliver to clients? Your goal is to have more people who have had a first-hand experience of you helping them so that they can then share that experience with others.

QUESTIONS FOR A ROOMFUL OF STRANGERS

- What brought you here today?
- How do you know <name>?
- Where have you traveled from today?
- What are you hoping to get out of this event?
- How did you find out about today's event?
- Do you attend many events like this?
- How are you enjoying the event?
- Is there anyone specific you are hoping to meet today?

The most important person in your life is *you*. To test this claim, remember back to your grade school class photographs. Whose was the first face you looked for?

This means that, when connecting with others, you need to understand that they are the most important people in their own lives. When given the choice, people look to do business with those they feel they know, like, and trust. Building these feelings is rarely achieved from anything you can say about yourself.

Decisions are made with emotion before logic, so the result you are looking to achieve is that it "feels right" to do business with you before you ever look for it to "make sense" to do business with you. The most successful approach you can take, to make progress in this area, is to understand that your prospect is the most important person in their life. By showing a genuine interest in them, you demonstrate a true level of connection with them, their situation, and their circumstances. This means asking questions and listening. Refrain from using their answer to a question to educate them on your similar experience. Instead, encourage them to share more details of their answer.

By listening intently, you are demonstrating that they are important to you, and this will help them feel good. Many service-based industries that rely on repeat business demonstrate this skill at a very high level. Examine the providers that you are most loyal to: places like your hairdresser, your local restaurant or bar, and perhaps even a taxi or car service. The chances are that your decision to continually do business with them is influenced by your feeling that they have a genuine interest in you.

Maintain eye contact in your conversations, repeat back what they have shared to show understanding, and catalogue key pieces of information that they share for you to bring back into future conversations and discussions.

WHAT'S IN A NAME?

The sweetest sound to any person anywhere in the world is the sound of their own name. You probably already know this and can recall dozens of moments when you have heard your name mentioned in a crowd or seen it written on a sign and could not help but be drawn toward it.

Remembering, recalling, and using the names of others is a great way of demonstrating your genuine care for other people. Think of the difference between someone saying "As your wife was saying" versus "As Charlotte was saying," or someone asking "How are the kids?" versus "How are Amelia and Emily?" This little adjustment changes everything. One is an attempt to show that you care, while the other is a demonstration that you have taken the time to care.

Remember the names of all of your important people, and then remember the facts of all that is important to them. Whether it is their family's names, pets' names, favorite sports teams, the school they went to, or the city they are from, if it is important to them, then make it important to you. Translating this information into future conversations, follow-up e-mails, proposals, and account management visits is a huge opportunity to stand out and make more of the opportunities that you create.

MAKING YOURSELF MORE MEMORABLE

In addition to remembering key facts about others, you probably want to make yourself more memorable to others too. Remembering names is not easy, but others remembering yours will certainly have an impact on your success. When you are meeting a stranger for the first time, there is a strong possibility that they will fail to catch your name because their mind is elsewhere in the split second that you share it. A very simple trick to increase your chances of being remembered by name is to slow the process down. When introducing yourself, you should give your name twice. First, you should give your preferred method of being addressed, followed by your full name, including your last name. This means that I introduce myself as "Phil, Philip Jones" and give others multiple opportunities to catch my name. It is simple and it really works.

BECOME THE EXPERT

If you are looking to create more opportunities, open more doors, and create a barrage of inbound inquiries, then you must be seen as the expert in your field.

The word *expert* may make you feel uncomfortable and could make you wonder how you could possibly position yourself as such. The little inner voice can easily start telling you that you haven't studied enough, learned enough, or simply don't yet know enough to be perceived as the expert.

When you take an honest look at your own experience, you can start to realize that there are many areas of your experience in which you have expansive expertise. Perhaps it relates to how your skill affects a certain group of people, perhaps it is a personal story associated with your profession, or perhaps it is even a very specific skill that is just a fraction of your overall work yet is something in which you hold a wealth of knowledge. Unlocking your expertise and positioning yourself as that person outwardly allows you to build your reputation quicker, establishes your authority, and starts more conversations with bigger potential customers.

Your goal is to become the x for y. Consider how much easier it is to become the expert as

- The accountant for dentists
- The real estate agent for investors in Houston
- The nutrition expert for busy moms

- The branding specialist for lawyers
- The logistics partner for eBay sellers

These specific micro-niches provide you with a razor sharp focal point to develop expert-based platforms that help create more opportunities. One of the fastest ways to be perceived as an expert is to be caught delivering presentations on your subject to audiences of potential customers. This instant leverage provides a wonderful lead-in for new sales opportunities. With the volume of events happening local to you, there are always opportunities for you to showcase your expertise.

There are many platforms from which you can share a powerful message that will have you be seen as the expert:

- Speaking at seminars and networking events
- Producing guest contributions for industry blogs and magazines
- Running teleseminars or webinars
- Participating in radio or television interviews
- Delivering podcasts
- Producing informational videos for YouTube

All of these media platforms are areas in which you can start delivering effective presentations in order to build your position as an expert in your area, grow your audience, create leads, and increase your sales.

BETTER THAN A BROCHURE

So many businesses continue to produce printed literature and brochures with the goal of supporting their sales efforts. I have no doubt that in certain industries a product catalogue is an essential tool. However, in many scenarios what is intended as an aid can quickly become a hindrance. In place of a brochure, and in particular when you have a service attached to your offering, it may be better to replace the printed literature that shares what you do with a useful tool that demonstrates the value you provide.

Examples of great brochure alternatives that build on your expertise would be

- A cheat sheet, checklist, or self-audit tool
- A sample pack of products
- A book or report written or compiled by you

These examples are often received as a gift by your prospect, are less likely to be disposed of, and carry far more value than a brochure. They provide visibility and credibility to you and your service, as well as create a leverage point for you to continue the conversation.

LET'S GET SOCIAL

Technology continues to move at a rapid pace, and staying in the game is a continual challenge for all of us. The biggest change I have experienced in my lifetime is the introduction and evolution of social media as a tool for communicating. A myriad of platforms exist that make it possible to reach and stay connected with literally millions of people across all parts of the globe. What is an incredible tool for expanding your business can also create a minefield of confusion for many sales professionals, as it becomes almost impossible to apply yourself and be true in all areas. These networks provide us with the tools to reach others, but they also provide others with the ability to reach, watch, and judge you, all without ever engaging in a physical conversation.

For those unaware of what the term "social media" relates to, it is the collective term for platforms such as Facebook, LinkedIn, Twitter, and YouTube. These forms of media are changing the way that we communicate. This shift in communications sounds drastic, and many of us are fearful of change—particularly when there is technology involved.

Social media is just modern-day "word of mouth," however, and is little different than what you have always done. This is about building relationships with your customers and community, as well as understanding what others are saying about you, to build your brand and grow your business.

Embracing this world can be highly lucrative, but it also comes with sizeable risks. Regardless of the platforms that you choose to use and how technologies evolve, this simple three-step formula will position you for sustainable sales success using social media:

1. **First impressions count**—Just like in the real world, you never get a second chance to make a first impression. Before you promote a profile, take the time to complete your profiles fully. Imagine that each profile is the equivalent of a retail shopfront, and be confident that it is representative of your current and future best self. Ensure that all biographies and details are current and represent you correctly, you have optimized the profile by linking them to other digital assets you may hold, and you have completed contact details in all appropriate areas.

   On all platforms, visual appearance is also critical. Be consistent with your branding, your colors, and the style in which you write. Make sure that any graphics you use are cropped to the correct size for the platform and display effectively on all major devices. Check the profile's appearance on desktops, laptops, tablets, and phones before promoting it to the world. Choose your photography to convey the precise impression you want to achieve in a new encounter. Most platforms are designed to be "social," so your outbound expression is likely to perform better as a human than a company name.

2. **Build an audience**—Once your profile is complete, it can be too easy to start sharing content and forget that without an audience your content is irrelevant. Your content and posts are important, but only when people are listening. Social media is particularly useful as a tool to communicate with the people who already know you, so start there. Most platforms provide a way for you to easily migrate contacts from elsewhere. If using it for business, then your first action should be to connect with as many of your existing customers and contacts as possible. Additionally, you should look to use all your current communication tools to let people know that you are active on social media. This means adding social media icons to your e-mail signature and stationery, informing all your customers when you write to them, making it a news story on your website and adding visual clues in any consumer-facing areas to encourage others to join the conversation on your chosen platforms. Make audience growth a key strategic action, and look to build your influence by proactively adding actions to your existing activities with this sole purpose in mind.

    Physically getting your customers to connect with your profiles is harder than just asking. Running a competition or great offer to reward them for visiting your profiles and connecting with you will drastically improve your chances. Remember that investing in this audience is critical to achieving social media success, since without an audience, your great work could easily be wasted.

3. **Communicate**—When it comes to content, the key is to remember that these are "social" platforms. Very few people are enjoying time on social media because they want to be sold to. To be interesting, you need to be varied with your communication and show yourself as human. If your message becomes monotonous, you become boring and people stop listening, so keep your outbound content varied. For me, this means creating content in the following areas:

   ○ **Educational**—Demonstrate your expertise by sharing self-created content using mixed media, such as blog articles, infographics, and videos. Also, share great content made by others in your space who have valuable information that would serve your audience. Delivering a mix of content that is both created and curated provides a valuable balance and also allows your content to be seen in the fine company of those whose you share.

   ○ **Engaging**—Social media is a tool to start and join conversations, so please make sure you are using it for such. Follow your clients, suppliers, and prospects and be sure to engage in their outbound communications. Similarly, produce posts and content that ask questions, encouraging others to add to it and join the conversation.

   ○ **Entertaining**—A big reason that many people invest time in following others on social media is the desire to be entertained. Share more of the real you by demonstrating some of your lifestyle, sharing your experiences, or showcasing hidden talents. Also, when you find something that tickles you, be ready to pass it on to your network, adding your own comments or commentary.

○ **Embarrassing**—Epic fails almost always create more engagement than illustrious success stories. Being prepared to share lighthearted embarrassing realities can keep the mood social, allows you to demonstrate a side to yourself that may not be seen in a typical corporate setting, and adds a level of humanity to you for your audience.

SOCIAL PROOF

It does not matter how good you are at something unless you have evidence of that reputation in a place where others can see it ahead of time. We live in a world where consumers have the power to make or break the success of a company based on how they decide to review and rate its offerings. It is your job to prove to your future buyers that you are highly competent in all that you do and to make it easy for them to place their trust in your hands by showcasing the positive experiences others have had in the past, proving you can help build a more successful future.

Sporting greats are judged by what they previously achieved, and teams recruit new coaches based on their previous results. The same can be said when people are looking for new suppliers. If you can demonstrate that you have done a fantastic job for others in the past, it goes a long way toward suggesting you will do a good job for them, too.

This is more than having testimonials hidden away on your website, in a filing cabinet, or in a folder in your bottom drawer, along with your customer letters. In today's age, social proof is one of the best convincers you have, and growing your social proof has become an essential part of sales success for many modern businesses. Most reviewed, five-star rated, award-winning, and best-seller status are all assets that allow you and your offering to stand out ahead of your competition. Using the words of others and third-party credibility allows you to be profound without being egotistical.

The distribution of your social proof is important. Before you can showcase it, you must ensure that you collect it. The trick here is quite simply to ask for it. We are all busy people, and taking the time to say nice things about each other, in a usable way, is rarely top of the list; therefore, we have to help it jump up the list.

Asking after you have delivered your product or service is likely to bring you a better response than after that moment has passed. Asking in a format that makes it easy for them is also highly likely to bring a better return. With so many formats for reviews, ratings, and testimonials, it can be easy to dilute your efforts by spreading yourself too thin. Choose the platforms that have the biggest impact on your business, and start by building solid proof of your services there first.

- Restaurants look to Yelp and OpenTable.
- Hotels and lodges may focus on TripAdvisor.
- Authors rely on Amazon reviews.
- Realtors may use Zillow reviews.
- Medical providers are on WebMD.
- Professional services could look to LinkedIn.

You must decide on the assets that are likely to serve you best and how you plan to use them to create more sales opportunities.

An example that I have employed successfully for many companies has been the collection and use of video testimonials. Just asking brings you huge results, but being prepared will help even further. The ability to record video on the spot allows you to act in the moment and capture powerful comments from existing clients when they are in the perfect moment to express their delight in your service. Be prepared with your equipment, have your questions ready, and make them feel at ease. It is better to record too much content than too little.

Once you get good at asking, you will have so much content that you'll want and need to get in front of people. Examples of how others have successfully used social proof to increase their sales success include:

- Adding client testimonials as references for future clients
- Pointing people who have contacted you by e-mail to your LinkedIn profile to read recommendations
- Showcasing awards and achievements in high-traffic customer areas
- Leaving written testimonials in a folder in the reception area of the office
- Using a quantity of reviews to increase visibility in searches
- Photographing written testimonials and posting them on your social networks
- Adding video testimonials to e-mail signatures and proposal documents
- Encouraging others to post their positive comments openly on social media
- Updating your website testimonials regularly and aligning specific recommendations to specific services
- Using the words of others in marketing literature

A simple lesson in all of the above is to put your social proof in front of as many people as possible. Linking your testimonials directly back to the source also adds to their authenticity and effectiveness in the decision-making process.

A Simple Script for Asking for Testimonials

"Hi (insert name), I was wondering if you could do me a small favor? (Pause and wait for positive response.) If you are happy with the work that we have done for you, then it would be a huge help if you would be kind enough to take a few moments and share it in writing. (Await positive response.) Thank you so much for that. We will obviously look to use your words in our marketing and share them with potential new customers. I look forward to reading your comments soon."

Giving Testimonials

Receiving testimonials is fantastic, but there is a lot to gain from giving them too. For each testimonial you produce, there is a strong possibility it may be used in someone's marketing, displayed in their workspace or shared with their network.

Take time to consider your words, and ensure that whoever comes into contact with your recommendation is aware of the people that you help and the problems that you solve for them. You may be surprised that sharing the value you received from working with someone else soon reciprocates in their network becoming more interested in you.

4

DEFINING YOUR SALES PROCESS

Garnering interest in you and your products or services is very different than creating intent in the buyer to move ahead with their decision. Successful selling starts with understanding that there is a process with a series of steps to work through if you are looking to achieve long-term success. Perhaps the easiest way to consider the process is to draw parallels with the dating game. Although dating is typically something people partake in with a predetermined future purpose, it is rare that communicating this purpose early will allow the relationship to go the distance and achieve the success desired. Slowing the process down often results in speeding the outcome up.

When you consider physical human relationships, then it becomes obvious that there are a number of steps that need to complete for the relationship to advance. The one critical step that is always important is to get to the position of "first date." This critical component is just as essential in the sales process as it is in the world of romance.

Knowing exactly how to sell is going to require you to become highly skilled at winning first dates. So far you have read about lots of ideas and strategies for creating opportunities, being prepared to look the part when the moments arise, and having your mind focused to impress when in the moment. It is now time to discuss precisely how you can define your process of creating the decision-making conversations that result in your first sale with a buyer.

It is highly unlikely that you are going to have a long-term profitable and successful relationship with a customer without a conversation taking place. A time-honored process that is unlikely to ever stop being true recognizes that:

- Questions create conversations.
- Conversations build relationships.
- Relationships expose opportunities.
- Opportunities lead to sales.

Your success in sales will be in direct correlation to both the quantity and quality of conversations that you start. If your goal is to win more business, then it starts with identifying your precise process to get in front of more of the right people.

PICK UP THE PHONE

Part of your job description as a professional salesperson is to interrupt someone's day long enough to uncover a challenge or opportunity they perhaps did not realize they had, identify your credibility in solving that challenge, and invite them to take a meaningful step toward that solution. Still one of the most powerful ways to start this exchange is by picking up the telephone to speak to your potential customer, with the goal of winning an appointment or further discussion to progress the opportunity.

If you are anything like me, then picking up the phone to talk to a complete stranger is not your favorite thing to do. When you look at cold-calling logically, it becomes easy to agree with some unquestionable truths:

- The call is quite likely to arrive at the wrong time for the recipient.
- The recipient is unlikely to be thinking of purchasing your product or service at that moment.
- They don't like receiving calls from strangers.
- Your interruption to their day is an inconvenience.

All of the above mean that your chances of success in this action are stacked against you before you even start. Therefore, playing the numbers game, rejection becomes the norm, and your confidence dwindles with each and every call.

Being professional means that making cold calls is entirely unnecessary. By thinking a little smarter, only ever calling people when you have a genuine reason to do so and looking to provide a consultative solution, you can soon make the phone your best friend.

Successfully starting an unplanned call is all about getting to a position of permission as quickly as possible after the call is answered. The standard structure that I teach to enable this follows three simple steps:

1. **Greeting**—A polite opening stating who you are
2. **Fact**—An undeniable, mutually agreeable piece of evidence to frame the conversation
3. **Question**—An easy-to-answer question that provides permission for the conversation to continue

Let's take a look back at the list we discussed in Chapter 1 and learn how you can use it to open your calls more effectively.

Friends—Your friends are all people who you are in contact with regularly. Contacting them by phone should be a regular occurrence, so picking up the phone in a professional context should be little extra challenge. An easy, rejection-free way of introducing your business to your friends is to ask in the third person. Instead of asking if they are interested, simply ask if they know someone who would be interested. They will often say themselves!

Example:

"Hi, it's Phil calling. I know that you have had a lot of success in your business, and I wondered if you would be open to helping me to grow mine?"

Records—All of the records you have gathered from previous roles you've had and events you've attended provide you with a simple reason to make contact. Reach out to someone and discuss the one thing you both have in common: the event or organization that resulted in you acquiring their records.

Example:

"Hi there! My name is Phil Jones. You probably don't remember me, but we met once at a Chamber event in Wisconsin. Are you still involved in the printing industry?"

Industry—Being an industry specialist always carries weight when you're making phone calls. The fact that you have experience in their industry and have worked with similar industries is often motivation enough for them to want to meet with you.

Example:

"Hi there! My name is Phil Jones. I saw your ad in the local trade magazine and thought that we may be able to help each other. How well has the ad worked for you so far?"

E-marketing—People who have submitted their details to connect with you online are very hot prospects and should be treated with respect. Remember to discuss what brought them to your website before discussing your products or services.

Example:

"Hi, it's Phil calling. You recently visited our website looking for more information about investment properties. I saw that you downloaded the e-book and just wanted to check in and confirm that it downloaded okay."

Networking—Appointment creation from networking is straightforward, because you are really having small appointments with everyone you meet. Often these meetings are simply a steppingstone to the true sales appointment. Use these events to win decision-making appointments, as opposed to selling at the events.

Example:

"It was great to meet you today, and it seems there is lots we could do to help each other. When is a good day of the week for us to catch up and continue the conversation?"

Directory—Phoning people from membership organizations and directories that you are part of takes a very simple introduction. You can simply open the conversation by discussing the organization that you are both a part of and move the conversation on from that point.

Example:

"Hi there! My name is Phil Jones, and I just saw you're listed as a member of the Self-Storage Association. We have recently become members, and I was wondering if you have ever attended the annual convention?"

Same name—Everyone you thought of in this section falls into one of the above categories. Pick up the phone, start the conversation, and see where it leads you.

These will still be challenging calls, but defining a specific reason or purpose for the call, in addition to introducing your products or services, makes the calls far easier, with less rejection and greater success.

Don't Leave Voicemails

When you make your outbound phone calls, it is highly possible that for a number of them you will be greeted by voicemail. My advice is to avoid leaving voicemail messages at almost all costs. Leaving a missed call alone is more likely to prompt a reply call than a voicemail. The second you leave a recorded message, you have handed the control in the conversation to the other party. Instead, hang up the call and attempt to reach them at another time, varying the time of day until you eventually reach them.

A Guaranteed Success Formula

A common wish of professionals is to spend all their business development activity with perfectly qualified prospects so that their time can be spent with people looking to buy and not with time-wasters. People try targeted advertising campaigns and volume direct mail to create opportunity; however, they are often disappointed with the response rate and the realization that there is no shortcut to success. Yes, these techniques have their place, and each brings a level of success; however, my biggest concern with these larger campaigns is not that they may not have the success rates anticipated, but more that if they do work, then the business may not be in the position to service the response.

When I question people looking for more customers, the desired growth rate in relation to number of customers is often a very sensible number. In most circumstances, just one or two new customers a week would revolutionize their success.

What could 100 new customers do for your business?

If this is a level of growth you are serious about, then I have a tried and tested strategy that significantly enhances your ability to win business and puts you in complete control of the process. First, you should consider three key concerns with looking for pre-qualified prospects:

1. They have already decided they are interested in the product and service, and hence have a strict brief for their requirements.

2. People will typically shop around; therefore, you do not have an exclusive opportunity.

3. You lose the control in the conversation because they require less consultation in providing their solution.

With this in mind, the job of persuading our prospects that they should do business with us can become extremely difficult, since they have too many preconceived ideas.

The alternative route to market is completely different. There is no fast track to the perfect opportunities, and often the missing ingredient to the success you desire is a little extra activity and a lot more direction.

- Take your list with at least 100 names on it.
- Make phone calls to arrange appointments with as many contacts as possible from your list, with the specific purpose of a brief exploratory meeting between two business professionals. Say you want to spend 15 minutes together to see how you can help each other.
- This should result in at least 10 appointments. In these appointments, first establish how you can help them. Then ask questions to establish what requirements they have for what you do and look for simple solutions. Do not try to sell to them. You are simply looking to establish whether there is a genuine business opportunity there.
- At least five of your meetings will highlight a requirement for what you provide. In those cases, say these words: "I am not sure if it is for you, but do you know anyone who ... ?" and introduce your products or services. Introducing your business in this way is completely rejection-free and makes it easy for your prospect to answer.
- When done right then, at least two of your prospects will go on to buy from you. However, the good news is that, by you doing it this way, those who don't buy will typically pass you to someone else who may. They find it easier to pass you on rather than give you a reason why they don't want to buy.

You then continue to repeat this process:

- Ten appointments
- Five genuine opportunities
- Two sales

The trick to this method is to simply get the appointment without being too prescriptive. Yes, you have a lot of meetings; however, if two new customers a week could change your business, then getting 10 appointments a week is surely worth it. They typically take less than an hour, and you may find just 10 hours a week is your very best investment.

SHOW THAT YOU CARE

There is a lot that we can all learn about customer service, but most of it is aimed at delivering great service after you have secured the customer. If you treat each of your potential customers as your "best" customer, there is every chance they will soon become your best customer.

I am confident that many of the most memorable gifts you've given throughout your life were those that were laced with thought and emotion, as opposed to significant financial expense. Winning a client is closely aligned with romancing a partner. Some of the simple actions that you can consciously commit to doing are as follows:

- Praise and compliment others.
- Offer support in times of trouble.
- Remember their important dates and events.
- Deliver random acts of kindness.
- Create introductions that could be valuable to them.
- Remember to say thank you in the right way.
- Open doors for others.

Having delivered and experienced dozens of ideas and campaigns to win the attention of prospects and clients, I've discovered there is one very practical idea that is easy to implement and brings consistent positive results year after year. As the world embraces more digital communication I foresee it only rising in effectiveness. Understanding that "it is the thought that counts," I wanted to find out the one form of communication that would guarantee my message was received, was high-impact, and delivered results.

The resulting communication tool that I've since developed is nothing more complicated than a handwritten card.

This simple piece of high-quality printed and folded card has delivered thousands of dollars in revenue to me as a universal tool to communicate with potential customers.

Success criteria for the cards my company produces are as follows:

- The card itself is blank inside so it can carry a personal hand-written message.
- The rear of the card carries basic contact details.
- The front of the card has a timeless and universal message.
- The envelope is brightly colored.
- The address on the envelope is handwritten.

The uses for these cards are almost limitless, and every one sent is almost certainly going to capture the attention of its recipient.

Examples of uses for your cards include

- Seeding a phone conversation with a potential prospect
- Following up from an unconverted sales conversation
- Acknowledgment of the impression someone made on you when you met networking
- Congratulations for success you witnessed them achieve
- A thank you for orders placed
- Gratitude for referrals passed

As an example, take a look at the card I sent recently to secure a very significant opportunity:

Dear David,

I have long been an admirer of your business and the great work that you do. I believe that I have a lot to offer the future success of your business and would love to talk further. I will be in touch shortly to see how we can help each other.

Thanks a million,
Phil

The other incredibly important difference between a card and a letter is that cards stand up and get displayed, while letters end up getting filed. This results in one being a referral generation tool for your business, while the other has very limited impact.

CHOOSE YOUR ALLIES

High on the priority list of every sales success campaign is the acquisition of new customers. Finding new prospects can be tiresome and lonely. A way for you to fast track this process and share the responsibility of new customer development is by partnering with other like-minded professionals who serve a similar customer base to you, are not direct competition, and can introduce you to their network.

The benefit of these partnerships is that they provide accelerated visibility into a new group of people, with the added authenticity of instant third-party credibility. They move you from looking to find your new customers individually to having the ability to locate them in multiples.

This approach has formed part of every business growth campaign that I have played a part in, both personally and with clients. The lesson was served strongest when we developed our property business. We had an investment property product that was an alternative to a pension, and it required the customer to make a fair-sized investment for some significant long-term rewards. Finding people for this product using traditional advertising and digital media was inconsistent and delivered very unpredictable results.

This led to us considering alternative ways to reach our ideal prospects. It became apparent that most of our potential customers were successful business owners and high-salaried employees who were already valuable customers of financial advisors, accountants, and attorneys. This allowed us to change our sales process entirely and take control of our results by forming countless small partnerships with these professionals who could introduce us to their customer base. Just imagine the difference it would make to your business if you were receiving dozens of referred appointments with personal recommendations....

Achieving this is within your control if you follow some simple steps:

- **Define your target market**—Understand exactly who your ideal customer is and what their current spending habits are.
- **Identify potential partner industries**—Take care to consider all potential product and service providers that already have a trusted relationship with your target market.
- **Make a list**—List the names and contact details of the people in the organizations you would like to speak with.

- **Create a win/win scenario**—Successful strategic alliances will only work if both parties are happy with the rewards for the effort. Financial reward is only one form of motivation, so consider what else you have to offer. Expertise, data, and introductions are all immensely valuable.
- **Create appointments to build relationships**—Get face to face with the people who you want to refer you and your business. People always prefer to introduce a human, rather than an organization. It is more rewarding for the introducer.
- **Look for first action**—It is easy, when discussing potential alliances, to get excited by the big picture. The idea will then "grow legs" and soon become a massive job. Experience has taught me that if you make the change too significant, nothing will happen. Therefore, start with something small. I typically look for just the first introduction.
- **Communicate like a pro**—When you receive introductions, you must understand that you are being trusted with someone else's most valuable asset. Act accordingly and communicate with your introducer every step of the way.
- **Say "thank you"**—Two of the nicest words to hear in the English language are "thank you." Take time to show your sincere gratitude for each introduction you are passed, regardless of results.
- **Overdeliver**—Whatever you promise to your introducer you must overdeliver on. A big goal is to get the contact to whom you were introduced to thank your introducer for the introduction. If you can gain this result, then expect a good number of further introductions.

Start thinking today about who could be passing you a steady stream of business, and start taking steps to develop powerful partnerships.

SOME SIMPLE TIPS

Throughout this chapter, there have been plenty of references to the importance of getting into scheduled sales conversations with your potential customers. This is always easier said than done, and securing someone else's time rarely occurs without challenge. In addition to the techniques already discussed, here are three more very practical strategies that deliver you the edge when it comes to creating appointments.

BE PRECIOUS WITH YOUR TIME

A mistake that many people make when looking to win appointments is that they ask for too long and appear to be too available. Decision makers are often swayed by intrigue, so if you are busy, giving the appearance of being in demand, they will be more motivated to see you for fear of missing out. When it comes to offering an appointment, you are more likely to win short appointments if you suggest times that indicate the meeting won't take long. By suggesting meetings at either 10 past the hour or 20 to the hour, you make it easier for them to find the time to fit you in. The assumption people make when asked to meet on the hour is that they require the full hour's availability to accept the meeting.

TWO VERSIONS OF YES

You should by now understand the importance of maintaining control in a conversation. Instead of offering your prospect the entire choice over their availability, an offer of two specific dates followed by the question "What suits you best?" typically results in you receiving a commitment to one of the two offered dates or them suggesting an alternative—resulting in you achieving the outcome of a confirmed appointment.

THE GUARANTEED APPOINTMENT There will always be occasions when winning that appointment continues to seem out of reach. Gatekeepers stand in the way and appointments continue to get rescheduled. One very special way of guaranteeing an appointment in any business-to-business environment is to become a customer of the company you would like to work with. Once you're a customer of theirs, you become remarkably more valuable to them and they are much happier to sit down with you.

This also means that it is well worth looking down your supplier list and seeing who could become a customer of yours. If you can turn your suppliers into customers, it can make for a massively increased value relationship.

5

MAKING THE MOMENTS COUNT

The time you spend in direct communication with your potential customer has the potential to be the most rewarding time invested in your business. Working so hard to create these situations means that you need to look at all of the factors that contribute toward your success in the moments you have created. Great products and services do not sell themselves. When given the opportunity to win the business, you should value it correctly and look to make the very most of it. In this chapter you'll discover strategies, tools, and techniques you can use to turn more of your contacts into contracts.

WHO HOLDS THE CONTROLS?

A common complaint about salespeople is that they are pushy. This description is often a result of an aggressive follow-up process and is entirely avoidable if you take a more professional approach.

By controlling the conversation process, you will very rarely find yourself needing to chase or follow up. In the event you find yourself in a situation requiring follow up, there are ways you can regain that control in a timely and comfortable manner.

Success in the sales process hinges on your ability to control your conversations and steer the thoughts and actions of the buyer. The aim of the game is to be in control throughout the journey and lead your prospect from inquiry through to decision, successfully navigating them through the maze toward the correct outcome to help them in their situation. A common mistake that many make is that they try to cheat on tried-and-tested practices by fast tracking. It's easy to believe that your potential customers are looking to make the purchase based solely on price and, on receipt of an inquiry, jump straight to a quotation. You then find yourself in a negotiation about price, an instant sale, or, worse still, complete silence and the end of a conversation. In most circumstances, your customers are looking to make their decision based on the entire value you provide and not just the price itself. One of the most valuable additions to your offer is you as a person, the human touch. Slowing the conversation down and helping them to get to know a little more about you keeps that in your control.

Knowing that people buy from people, you can avoid difficult follow-up scenarios if you start by building a relationship. Where possible, do this face to face. During this meeting you will build rapport and ask questions to equip yourself with the information you need to make a recommendation to your potential customer. It is at this point, however, that simple mistakes can be made.

Ask questions and listen. Avoid overcommunicating, and learn everything you can about their circumstances.

Some of the best advice I received as a young salesperson was about the importance of listening. Great questions are essential, but if you don't listen to, or benefit from, the answers, then you will never get the maximum benefit from your opportunities. Being a great sales professional has nothing to do with having the "gift of the gab" or "having all the answers." Success can be maximized by asking great questions and listening to the responses.

Listen is an interesting word as it shares the exact same letters as the word *silent*. Sometimes that's what listening is: saying nothing at all and allowing your potential customer to continue to share information. Take time to listen and write notes. By really listening, you will hear things that allow you to tailor your recommendations better to their needs, as well as identify countless more opportunities for both now and in the future.

The goal is to put yourself in a position where you can deliver your recommendations in person and not by mail or e-mail. This means that if you are not in the position to deliver your recommendations in the first meeting, you should arrange a meeting to discuss your findings before leaving and place yourself in the position of controlling the next conversation. Securing the second date while still in the first is far easier than trying to pin it down at a later date.

Upon returning with your recommendations, start by rebuilding the value of the position you held when you left the last meeting. Reconfirm your customer's requirements and then walk them through your recommendations, explaining exactly how you can help them and ensuring they see everything they are getting for their money. Your role is to give them all the information they need to make a decision before asking them to take the next step.

By inviting people to make a decision in the moment, you can eliminate the need for a follow-up call. The time you invest in controlling this process at the beginning will reward you immensely in improved conversion rates and in less time spent chasing decisions.

Gaining decisions in person is always the goal, but there almost certainly will be times when this is not possible. Your objective is to be involved in the conversation in which the decision is being shared. If you cannot get face to face, then alternatives include scheduled phone calls and video conferencing. However, sometimes you still find yourself faced with the need to send your offer of service and then follow up with the goal of progressing the sale. If this happens, follow these simple tips to increase your results in follow up:

- Don't leave voice mail messages. Leaving a message prevents you from calling again.
- Open your call by checking they received your recommendations (not "quote" or "proposal").
- Ask them "What questions do you have?" The answers they give here put you back in control. If they have any questions, your answer can lead to a decision. No questions means a decision has been made.
- If the first form of communication fails, then try something different. Don't harass.
- If it's worth it, then visit to see them face to face.
- Take your offer away by making it time dependent. It's just like telling a child they'll get no dessert if you have to remove their uneaten dinner. Limiting your offer can have the same result.

Remember, the biggest reason people do not buy from you is that they remain undecided. Everybody who is stuck in indecision will at some point decide, so if your follow up remains unproductive, don't just stop. Keep these people on a NNT (No Not Today) list and periodically check in with them, add them to your newsletter, and make a personal note in your schedule to revisit in the future. At some point their circumstances will change and they may just need your help. Persistence has certainly proved successful for many before us, and I am sure it will continue to bear fruit in the future.

EASY FIRST YES

Big decisions are hard to make. Getting customers to make them can be slow, laborious, and complex. When a customer is looking for a new supplier, they have many decisions to make, but perhaps the most important question they ask is "Why you?" This question is rarely answered before a decision is made.

Referrals, testimonials, and third-party stories can all add to a consumer's confidence in choosing you, yet still, a decision that involves significant change can be a difficult process for the consumer to navigate. Imagine if you were looking to change from a long-term and trusted supplier or had an immediate need for a large project. Choosing whom to give your business to becomes a heavy task, and the bigger the decision, the harder it becomes to make.

However, you can often speed up the decision-making process and win more new customers by making their first step a simple one. Let me demonstrate with a very simple example that I imagine is familiar to you. I am sure that you will have eaten in a restaurant—a great industry full of examples of easy first yeses. What they are looking to secure is the maximum transaction value per table, and so they try to sell drinks, appetizers, more drinks, main courses, more drinks, desserts, and coffees to all customers. Instead of adding all these decisions ahead of time, what they do first is sell table reservations and market key offers to fill those tables. They know that when they fill the tables, they have more chances of selling the food and drinks at various stages throughout your stay. Take a look at your process and see if you are trying to sell the whole meal in one go. Just like in a restaurant, it is difficult to decide on a dessert until after you have finished your main meal.

Great examples of easy first yeses are low-priced initial transactions that turn your prospects into customers quickly and easily.

- A website developer offering a low-priced audit ahead of rebuilding a site
- A landscaper providing fixed-price lawn care before a maintenance contract
- A construction worker conducting a small repair or handyman job before quoting for the major project
- A CPA helping file your tax return before offering to help with your ongoing financial planning
- A direct sales representative showcasing their products before inviting you to join the business

Continuing the analogy of the dating game, this is the equivalent of inviting your partner to take a vacation with you before you ask them to move in with you.

By breaking bigger decisions into smaller steps, you can often gain a very quick decision from your prospect, have them experience working with you, and side-step all of your competition by making yourself the easy choice.

WHAT SELLING REALLY IS?

In the medical industry, it is often said that "prescription before diagnosis is malpractice." Imagine if you visited your doctor and, without asking a single question, the doctor launched into an explanation of how wonderful this new drug was and encouraged you to take the pills twice a day. I imagine you would be a little confused and less than confident about following the recommendations of your doctor.

As an alternative, if the doctor were to sit you down, learn about your symptoms, run some tests, and then make the exact same recommendation, your confidence in following the advice would be significantly greater.

My personal definition for selling is "earning the right to make a recommendation." This means that you should never introduce your offer of a product or service without having a confirmed, customer-centric reason first. Your framework for recommending anything to anyone should always be "Because of the fact that you said ABC, what we recommend is XYZ." This structure means that a large part of every sales conversation is focused on you gathering evidence to support your recommendation.

PROD THE BRUISE

Questions are so important in stopping you guessing and ensuring that you earn the right to recommend your products and services. Typically, the reason for any sales opportunity not being maximized is that the questions were either missing or inappropriate.

Understanding that people make buying decisions based on emotion and not logic, it is paramount that you get your prospect to share emotion during your questioning. A tried and tested approach to nearly every sales opportunity is to follow this simple three-stage questioning technique.

1. **What is your plan … ?** Start with a big and broad question that encourages your buyer to share their vision for the future. In my business I typically start by saying quite simply "So explain to me the plan for the business." The result

of this question is often 15 minutes of communication that gives me the big picture and includes the business owner's goals. The key is to keep the question broad and not specific. Your product offering will only affect part of the plan; however, not understanding all of it makes it difficult to understand where your part fits in. A further factor in this opening question is the knowledge that most people are optimistic about their future and believe that it will be a better spot than where they are today. Anchoring the basis of your recommendation to their future successes allows for you to think bigger and for them to act braver. Throughout this series of questions, be looking first for the "what" and then the "why." If the plan includes luxuries, get specifics, because these become very valuable when closing.

2. **How will you feel … ?** Once you understand where they are going, it's important to understand how they will feel when they get there. This is simple; you just need to ask … and then listen. You need to be prepared to dig a little here to get to the real emotions that make this technique really powerful. You are looking to evoke extreme emotions like pride and euphoria. Encourage strong adjectives, and don't accept simple answers like "I will feel pretty good" or "Okay."

3. **What are the consequences of not … ?** Steps 1 and 2 are positive and uplifting, and they also provide the foundation and the contract to create the impact of this third part. Many people are significantly more motivated to avoid a loss than to make a gain. Allowing your prospect to honestly consider the negative of not achieving their objective in direct contrast to their previous thoughts and feelings provides you with a powerful platform to recommend from. Most people

don't give sufficient consideration to failure, and asking this question forces them to think about it. Once people have visualized failure, they will work far harder to avoid it.

This technique works by establishing your prospect's plans, elaborating on the success of achieving these plans, and then visualizing the pain of failure. I often describe it as painting a picture of Utopia for them, checking their feelings, and then finding their pain and aggravating it a little. The good news is that once you have prodded the bruise enough, your presentation should be the best ointment for that bruise, and if you get these processes right you will win more business.

Great questions allow you to stop selling and start recommending.

MAKE IT EASY TO BUY

The main function of a salesperson is to encourage customers to purchase goods or services. I often refer to salespeople as professional "mind-maker-uppers." If you are looking to help your prospects reach decisions, then you really should take a look at your processes and ensure you are doing all you can to make buying a painless process. Consider every barrier that exists to doing business with you and look to remove it. Revisit your paperwork process, pricing structure, and onboarding process, and do all you can to simplify and take away any unnecessary effort from the consumer.

With online retailers conditioning buyers with the simplicity of "one click to buy" and forms being filled in within seconds from our computers' memories, it is your job to make the process of doing business with you as pain free and effortless as possible for your buyer. Remove the barriers and do as much of the work for them as possible. In addition, adding factors that cause you to share the risk with the customer means that you can gain their commitment with less resistance.

Examples of risk reversal include

- Money-back guarantee
- Free initial period
- No success, no fee
- No contract
- Guaranteed results
- Attractive payment terms

If you are looking for more business, I encourage you to remove all obstacles from your buying process and continue to make your own luck.

PUT A BOW ON IT

If you provide a service, as opposed to a range of products, it is likely that many of your customers avoid consulting you because they don't know exactly what they want, they are unsure what they may have to pay, and they do not wish to end up confused or embarrassed. It can be greatly beneficial for service providers to think more like retailers. If you owned a shop with items that had no prices showing, a browsing customer might assume that everything in the shop was too expensive, and you would run the risk that they would not ask for assistance for fear of embarrassment.

Imagine yourself again as a retailer. Your aim is to encourage people to go into your store and increase footfall. Service-based industries have the same goal and can use three simple techniques to help customers do business with them more easily.

1. **Price primers**—Provide an example of a service in a way that explains your total pricing strategy to customers. Major supermarket chains use value products to do this, and the automotive industry may use a range of cars. The process involves taking a snapshot of one service and putting a price on it, as it will educate your audience about your overall pricing strategy. Being proud of this price demonstrates the value you believe it offers and allows customers to get a feel for your market position.

   Examples include

   - An accountancy service placing fixed monthly pricing on three tiers of service
   - A domestic cleaning company having a fixed fee for a one-bedroom apartment
   - A realtor having a fixed fee for an apartment listing
   - A architect placing a price on a set of approved drawings for an extension
   - A hairdresser locking down the price for a blow-out

   These uncomplicated single-price offers allow people to decide whether they can afford you, provide benchmarks for variations, and give the buyer confidence to engage in conversation with you without fear of embarrassment.

2. **Bundled offers**—Value is merely a perception. By creating a bundle of components within a service offering, you can demonstrate a far stronger position in your buyer's mind for all that you are worth. The minute the buyer can clearly correlate a time for money calculation, they cannot help but judge you based on how much you are charging per hour, and this can sour a business relationship. Create collections of products and services that demonstrate

great value, increase your average transaction value, and allow you to deliver a more complete service to your customer.

When putting your bundle together, consider all that you can include—not only the tangible services or products, but also those that add value, such as customer care, service expectation, and telephone and e-mail support, all of which add substance.

Examples include

- A design agency bundling a suite of services as a "business in a box," including the design and production of a full complement of stationery, a basic website, and a brand guidelines package aimed at new business start-ups
- A health and nutrition reseller creating a pampering set by combining a number of best-selling products, and creating gift hampers for calendar events
- A wedding venue bundling a fixed-price service that includes food, drinks, photography, and entertainment

3. **Monthly payment**—Most people are concerned less with an overall price and more about the fee for each month. Personally and professionally, it can be typical for people to have a monthly overhead that they consider. Aligning your offering with their buying habits can make decision making easier.

Typically, if you can turn a large pay-in-arrears product or service into a sustainable pay-monthly option, the results are increased profit, improved cash flow, and maximum customer retention. If you are not offering your clients a packaged pay-monthly service, you may well be missing out on a massive opportunity.

Examples include

- Pay-monthly credit options for high-value goods
- An attorney offering a monthly service plan with agreed service levels
- A personal trainer creating a rolling monthly fee for a package of monthly services

Try packaging up your services and offering a monthly payment plan to win new customers and develop a steady stream of recurring revenue.

CHOOSE YOUR WORDS

If you are familiar with my previous work *Exactly What to Say*, you will already be aware of the importance of using the right words at the right time in order to achieve the right results. Yes, words do matter, and just as the correct words help your sales success, there are many words that have the exact opposite effect.

The worst time to think about the things you say is in the moment you are saying them. I highly encourage you to learn more about the power of your words. Quite often the difference between somebody choosing you, choosing somebody like you, or choosing to do absolutely nothing is down to you knowing exactly what to say, when to say it, and how to make it count.

With that in mind, it's probably important that we try to make more of our conversations count. Instead of telling you what to say, let's look at some of the common mistakes people make that negatively affect their sales success.

Let's explore the impact of just seven independent word choices that make their way into your daily conversations. If you can remove them, replace them, or change them, or at least understand what they are doing, then you can control more of your outcomes.

IF

The first word is a simple two-letter word that can help people decide whether they are in your camp or out of it, whether they believe you or not, whether they are thinking that it is something for them or not for them.

The two-letter word in question is "if." As children, we learned to speak first by understanding objects. We then saw those objects as pictures, and we associated each picture with a sound, a spoken word. The word that sound made allowed somebody to know that we wanted the object. Once we understood the sound, the next thing we understood was the word, and eventually we could write that word.

As adults, we do things in the complete opposite way. We see a word on paper or hear a word in conversation, and the next thing we do is associate that word with the image it recalls in our memory. Pictures are what drive decisions. Everything that anybody decides to do, they are deciding to do for at least the second time, because first they decided to do it in their mind before they ever took action.

The word "if" creates a choice. "If" creates a question, and when faced with a question, people decide which side of that question they land on. So what you are doing when you use the word "if" in your sales conversations is creating a condition. People see the picture of the condition you have presented and decide instantly what side of that condition they fall on.

Here is an example. Say you said to someone "If you knock that glass over, the wine may stain the carpet." They make an instant decision based on how likely they are to be clumsy and either accept or decline your information. You have a 50/50 chance of any advice you offer being taken.

Swapping the word "if" with the word "when" creates a completely different reaction and results in the other person being only able to see the stain in their mind. They are far more likely to act on the advice you share.

The lesson in this example is even bigger than the obvious. Instead of talking in terms of "if," which is future and conditional, when you move your conversations to "when," you move them to the present and make them active, hence massively increasing your chance of success.

But

The second word for your consideration is one that is overused and tremendously damaging to many a conversation—including the conversations you have with yourself and your teams. The word is "but." Think of the times you have heard this word in conversation. Perhaps you received some feedback delivering praise and recognition before it was followed up with a "but." The only part you remember clearly is everything that followed the "but." The word almost negates anything that was said prior to it and is associated with nothing but bad news. Please don't think you can change the word to "however"; this achieves nothing other than using more syllables.

Swap the word "but" for the word "and," resulting in all of the information now holding true.

Example:

> "We would love to work with you and can see how it would benefit you, but we really need to talk about the pricing."

> "We would love to work with you and can see how it would benefit you, and now just need to talk about the pricing."

These two examples say almost exactly the same thing. It is just that the first has a sprinkling of confrontation and the second has an abundance of collaboration.

Swap "buts" for "ands" to see your conversations become more inclusive and gain you more of what you want.

Cost

This third word has the ability to make me squirm and should be banned from every single commercial conversation on earth. Many four-letter "C" words are inappropriate in public, and this one causes the most damage. How do you feel about the costs in your life? Are they good things or bad things? Almost always, the costs in your life are things that you see as bad things. The second you label the value you are looking to bring to a customer with a cost, you instantly destroy that value you have been building and associate your offering with a description that means money out for little in return.

My guess is that if you are asking to be paid for your goods or services, then you are planning to bring your customer something in return for that payment. Perhaps they receive a time saving, a financial benefit, or even just a valuable experience—whatever these returns are, they change the label you can attach to your offering. If you are offering something in return for payment, then you have the option to label it as an investment. Typically, people are far prouder of their investments than their costs. My advice to you is to change your language from "cost" to "investment" when speaking with your customers. When you change what you call it, you change how people perceive it.

WE

Just another two-letter word, massively overused when explaining how you work, the time you have been doing it, and your unique attributes that have you positioned as the number one choice. It appears in sales literature, on websites, and in spoken word. The word is *we*, and its extensive overuse results in you literally "we"-ing all over your customers.

When you talk from a position of "we," then the primary beneficiary of the information and the attachment to the receipt of the outcome stays with the person who is communicating. The word "we" talks in terms of your interests and not your customer's or prospect's and is unlikely to inspire them to action. Shift the positioning around as often as you can. When you see or hear the word "we," change it to the word "you."

When you say things like "What we provide is a comprehensive training program with a three-year guarantee, service plan, and extensive warranties," this keeps you in possession of the thing you are looking for them to purchase. Swap the beneficiary and activate the sentence. Instead of "What we provide," move it toward "Choosing us means you benefit from . . . ."

It should never be about what "we" have on offer when the recipient is expected to be "you." Place your customer in possession of your goods or services with words, and then when you invite them to accept your offer, they are far more likely to move forward.

EXPENSIVE

This is less likely to be a word you use yourself, yet it is potentially something your client could use to describe you or your service, so it needs to be realigned promptly to prevent unnecessary damage. If a customer or prospect labels you as "expensive," it will be almost impossible to get them to see your product or service as something for them to purchase.

The term itself can only exist in relation to something else and needs comparisons. Its use means that your buyer already has existing judgments about the price you are asking, and the label they have applied is anchored on some other existing data. Think to yourself, "is a Rolls Royce expensive?" You may well think yes, and compared to most of the Ford model range, it absolutely would be. Yet when compared to a Bugatti, the said Rolls-Royce is actually kind of inexpensive. Instead of calling something expensive, let's just shift it, change the word, call it something different. To the person who's labeled our thing as expensive, we talk about it as a premium option.

Buying the "expensive" option can have you feeling like you received a bad deal. Choosing the "premium" option feels luxurious and informed.

CHEAP

The next word is on the other side of that fence: *cheap*. If someone describes something as cheap and something else, the word that follows "cheap" is certainly not something you'd like to be associated with yourself, your company, your products, or your services. So let's ban the word cheap, too. We may well have in our product portfolios things that are less expensive than those premium options, but this does not mean that they are cheap. I expect they're still great at what they do, and in fact, what they do is deliver great value.

Take your lead from some of the major supermarket chains, some of the biggest brands out there, and swap "cheap" for the word "value" or perhaps even "essential." Allow the buyer to be prouder of their entry-level purchase.

PROBLEM

Talking about the "problems" you see with others will win you about as many friends as telling someone they have an ugly baby.

By labeling somebody else's circumstances this way, you can create a defensive feeling in the buyer, and the result can be catastrophic. The reality is likely to be that they had some strong involvement in creating the very thing you are labeling as a "problem" and their sense of responsibility encourages them to stand by it.

Challenges can be overcome. They are obstacles that you can move out of the way, step over, side step, move around … whatever it is you might do, but problems are going to cause arguments. Challenges can be resolved and achieve positive results from forward thinking instead of blaming and negatively labeling.

For each of these words, the primary shift is to move conversations away from a focus on you selling the product or service and toward your buyer owning the item or outcome.

INSTEAD OF THIS:	SAY THIS INSTEAD:
If	When
But	And
Cost	Investment
We	You
Expensive	Premium
Cheap	Value
Problem	Challenge
When I sell	When you own

Your Sales Presentation

Often referred to as the pitch, the presentation part of the sales process is the piecing question—the part where we wrap up the decision that we're looking for the other person to make in as neat a package as possible and then ask them to make that big decision.

Many aren't comfortable with the word *pitch*. To me, it grates a little. We're all professional at what we do, so what we're doing is presenting the outcome we're looking for, not pitching it.

Before I explain what should go into a presentation that gets you the results you're looking for, it is important to understand where we should be positioning this within our sales process. A sales presentation should largely be one-way traffic. You should already know that your outcome is right for the customer: you would have prepared to understand the prospect, built rapport and trust, and asked some questions. This qualifies that what you're about to present to them is going to fit their needs and be a fitting solution to their challenge, so they can end up saying the words "Thank you" to you at the end of your presentation.

Having got all of that work out the way, you should be pretty confident about the fact that your presentation is going to lead toward a "Yes!" It means you're in complete control and can deliver a sales presentation purely as one-way traffic, with little to no interruptions, that allows you to get through all of the information, transferring enthusiasm and building momentum toward your close.

You are looking for people to make a decision and commit to moving forward. Enthusiasm itself is a catalyst to a decision, so if you're looking for people to be decisive and feel excited about it, you've got to be excited about it too. Be enthusiastic in your delivery of the solution.

The presentation is largely you—not a slide deck or a beautiful brochure or a product sample. You are the presentation. Those tools can support your presentation, but they should not lead it. Every great sales presentation, whether it's a 60-second elevator pitch, the closing remarks of a half-day tender, or the summary of a face-to-face meeting, should follow a structure that's delivered on purpose.

Before leading into a presentation, decide what you want people to do as a result of listening to what you have to say. Are you looking for them to say yes and sign a contract? Are you looking for them to hand over a check or cash or give you their card details? Are you simply looking to get into the next stage in the process, or are you looking for some further information? Until you know the answer to that question, you cannot build a winning sales presentation.

There are three stages that need to go into making a show-stopper presentation.

THE BEGINNING

This set-up has two key components:

1. **A scene setter**—An opening statement that affirms for them exactly why the conversation is happening. It might be something as simple as, "The reason that we're here today is to look at how XYZ service can help improve ABC." Very quickly, you demonstrate that this is an outcome-focused conversation. Bringing it back to a purpose regains the control for you. You have to make that crystal clear from this preliminary moment, and by reading their body language and the way they react to that statement, you will realize how much work is left to do. If they nod and

smile back at you, they've accepted the fact that's exactly the purpose of the meeting and they're comfortable. If, however, they sit uncomfortably, it may suggest that they were just looking for information or are not even in the position to buy today, in which case you know that your presentation has to deliver at a far higher level.

2. **An agenda**—This could be a written formalized agenda, handed to each participant, that tells people the points you will be covering, or it could simply by a verbalized statement explaining what you are about to cover. Spoken, it may be as simple as, "Let's take a little time to recap our history, how we're equipped to help you achieve your goals, and the specific service recommended to you today, and then I'll leave time for you to make a decision about what you would like to do next."

By delivering an agenda on that basis, you gain permission to control the discussion and follow the tracks laid down. By telling people there's going to be a decision asked for at the end, you have warned them. It also means that you have obligated yourself to ask for the decision at the end of the presentation by seeking it at the start.

THE MIDDLE

The middle is important because this is where you are required to provide people with enough information to make a buying decision. There are three key components that need to go in the middle of every presentation:

1. **History and credibility**—This is both you and your company. You are looking to distinguish yourself from your competitors, and this is your chance. This is how long

you've been doing what you do and the types of people that you've worked with in the past. Examples of things that bring instant credibility are

- Number of successes in your past
- Awards and accreditations
- Name drops from high-profile clients or partners

Be careful, when sharing your awesomeness, that you are not dismissive of other clients. Don't just drop the name of your biggest and best clients if you're speaking to somebody who's far smaller than those people, because they may well be thinking, "Well, if you work with big companies like that, you're too big for me. I don't want to be your worst customer." Developing a "from" and "to" could help you in that statement. In my business, I work with hundreds of independent home-based business owners right through to Fortune 500 companies. This brings confidence to people of all levels that we are a good fit for them.

Credibility can also be built with inclusive statements made in the third person. Sometimes it is difficult to blow your own trumpet, and shifting your testimonials and client feedback into third person allows you to deliver a more humble brag.

Examples:

- "Many of our customers describe us as … "
- "Just last week one of my customers said … "
- "If you look at our profile on Yelp, you will see over a hundred five-star reviews."

By including third-party endorsements in your history and credibility statement, you add value and substance, and they can be delivered effortlessly without making you sound arrogant.

2. **Share the range of products and services that you offer**—Have you ever had a prospect tell you, despite you being able to offer that product or service, that they're buying it from somebody else? It surely has to be your responsibility to share everything you have to offer, and even though it might be in your brochure or on your website, still, this is your chance to tell people. This is no more than a shopping list of products and services—not a detailed description of everything you have. With a handful of services, a list may suffice. If it's more of a comprehensive offering, then a "from" and "to" gives the buyer confidence that you have them covered. Not only does this plant seeds for future sales opportunities but it can also give the buyer confidence in today's transaction by knowing that you can grow with them.

3. **Wrap up just the one thing that you're looking for them to make a decision on today and dress it up in how it could be beneficial to them**—People can make only one decision at a time. You have to sell the key item before you can sell any of the extras, so give them all the information they need to know about that one thing. This is in terms of the item's features, but it's also what it means to them and how that can help them in their circumstances. Use words like "because of the fact that you said," insert their words back in and then explain what that means to them in terms of how your solution could help their circumstance.

At this point you should also be proudly addressing the price of your offering and not saving it until the very end. The price is perfectly positioned following your explanation of the entire package, and your lead-in to the price could be as simple as "You receive all of that for a fixed investment of just (insert price)."

THE END

There'll be parts of the middle where the prospect stops listening, and you might think "But why would somebody stop listening to me in the middle of the most important part of my presentation?" You might even be thinking it's because they're not interested. The reality of it is it's probably quite the opposite. They've gone off to a happy place and have started to think about the implications or how to implement the ideas that you're looking for them to employ. Because they've stopped listening, when you come back around to capture their attention, they'll wonder what they've missed and won't feel like they have all the information they need. Therefore, they can't be asked for a decision yet, which is why you need a strong ending.

Give them a summary. All that the summary consists of is outlining what you've told them. Recap the fact that you've shared your history and your credibility, you've shared the range of products and services that you offer, and you've talked to them in detail about the one thing that's right for them and why you think that's the case. Mentally they'll start to tick those things off and discover they've received all the information they need. Because they then believe they have all the information they need to make a buying decision, you can do what you said you were going to do in the beginning and ask them for that decision. Then close by leading them toward the outcome that you predetermined at the start, and invite them to take the next step.

It is likely you will be required to give variations of this presentation on countless occasions in your lifetime. Your words matter, and at this point of interaction they matter more than ever. Write your sales presentation out word for word, consider the components as independent building blocks, and continue to grow in confidence and competence as your sales presentation evolves in each and every exchange.

CLOSING THE SALE

So much pressure can be put on the seller to "close the sale." This pressure is largely unnecessary if you have followed the principles that I've shared so far in this book. A close is simply an invitation to the buyer to take an action that confirms their decision. Given the context that has bought you to this point in conversation, asking for a decision seems more than fair. You are best to detach yourself from the success of the decision itself. Know that your responsibility is to help the buyer conclude their action with a decisive response and to facilitate that decision-making process. Let go of the thought that you are manipulating or demanding a positive decision, and instead see yourself as guiding the outcome toward what you feel is the right solution for all parties. Buyers are typically looking to be led, and the close is your demonstration of leadership that results in everyone achieving what they came for. To help you navigate this part of the conversation, next are five widely used techniques that allow you to control the end of a discussion and lead toward the finish line.

BEING ASSUMPTIVE

Throughout all we have shared so far, you have been exposed to a very consultative sales process. A big reason many people become scared of asking for the business is fear of rejection. Adding an assumptive close to your consultative process is the one technique that is completely rejection free.

Knowing that your buyer is probably looking to you for guidance, you can make a series of statements and follow those statements with a question. If the buyer then answers that question, it means they are happy with the statements you've laid out.

Taking this out of context, imagine a social telephone conversation that plays out like this:

> "We have been looking to find a date in our schedules that works best for our next night out and realized that Thursday the twenty-third looks best. I was thinking we would eat first at the Chinese place on the hill at around seven p.m. and then head to the new cocktail bar downtown for nine-ish. To get to the restaurant, will you be driving or taking a taxi?"

This is a series of statements that then results in the recipient answering with either option and agreeing to the rest of the agenda. The only other options are to suggest an alternative or ask a question. Every way around, it is a fast and effective way of confirming a decision.

It takes confidence and posture to deliver this effectively. To help your confidence in delivery, consider the work invested to get to this point. No doubt your prospect is very interested and has nodded and smiled all through your presentation. I promise at this point you have earned the right to be assumptive.

A simple business example would be as follows:

> "We will make a start on your project straight away and expect to have it completed no later than the middle of next month. Inclusive of everything we have discussed today, your investment is just $450, and to get things started I have a simple one-page form to complete that starts with your name and address. What is the best address for you?"

The second they answer the question, they have agreed to the prior statements and have, therefore, confirmed the order. The only action your customer can take, as an alternative, is to ask you a question. If they do, simply answer the question and then reiterate your simple closing question.

THE CONDITIONAL CLOSE

I am sure in the past you have been asked by a customer to move from your standard pricing, terms and conditions, or timelines. Whenever a customer asks you to alter your standard terms, before considering your move you should regain control with a conditional close. A conditional close is based on the structure "If I can … , will you … ?"

Examples include:

- "If I can secure that price, will you be ordering today?"
- "If I can meet your delivery deadlines, will you pay today?"
- "If I can change those terms for you, will you commit to us as an exclusive supplier?"

Shifting the control back in this way means that you only have to give something away in return for an action from them. It can help bring scenarios to decision quickly, and it allows you to find out if your prospect actually has the intent to transact at all or is simply shopping around.

THE ALTERNATIVE CLOSE

Earlier in the book you learned about how the alternative close can be used to secure appointments more easily by giving a choice of two dates and then asking, "Which one suits you best?"

The exact same principle of delivering the customer a perception of choice by offering multiple variations of a "yes"-based answer can allow for decision making to be accelerated. Pick details from the entire transaction and use the choice of these details to help gain clarity over the entire decision.

Examples include:

- "Would you like it in the red or the black?"
- "Is it going to be with or without the (insert item)?"
- "Would you be looking for delivery on a weekend, or would midweek work?"

Limiting the choices and ensuring you stay in control is what steers the decision making promptly. Give stark contrasts and avoid ambiguity. Taking the first example, had I asked, "What color would you like?" the customer could have then spent an eternity discussing the plethora of choices and prolonged the decision with too many choices to make.

THE DIRECT CLOSE

I am sure that you have had times in your career when you have had dealings with people you just couldn't get a decision from. Perhaps they have asked you to revise your proposals time and time again and have been in your "maybe" pile for what seems like an eternity. I refer to these people as "faffers," and it is our job to bring these people to a decision quickly and efficiently. Your time is precious, and in these scenarios the direct approach is really the best option. I would only ever use this approach if I were comfortable in receiving a "no" response from the prospect.

This means presenting the buyer with a "yes" or "no" option with phrases like "Are you going to place an order? Yes or no?"

Your confidence in this process triggers a decision, and either way you can move forward. This can often result in a positive decision, since the fear of you taking the offer away can regularly trigger a buying decision.

THE SUMMARY CLOSE

Big decisions are hard to make. Small ones can be easier. Breaking the decision down by presenting your buyer with a series of small questions that help them find confidence over their decision is a wonderful second attempt if they remain indecisive.

Your goal is to build a rhythm of questions that all lead toward yes-based answers. The rhythm of the buyer confirming "yes" to each component results in the yes option being the only option for the whole thing. Start with guaranteed yeses and build to the more specific decisions as you go.

An example for an accountant could be:

- "So you definitely need an accountant?"
- "And you have a tax return due next month?"
- "You would like the accountant to be local?"
- "And capable of dealing with your entire accounting needs?"
- "We have chatted today, so do you believe that we can help you with what you need?"
- "You understand our service levels and pricing?"
- "And based on our discussions, we believe the silver package would work best?"
- "And this is something you would like us to get started on straight away?"

Gaining a positive response to each component answer builds confidence in all parties and allows you to move to the precise next action required to get started.

This slowed-down and component-led approach also allows you to locate a smaller stumbling block that you may be able to work around once it's isolated.

BUYING TRIGGERS

There are many factors that trigger people into making buying decisions. Adding these elements to your presentations, recommendations, and closes can provide the special edge that is an additional catalyst for the decision:

- Scarcity of product
- Limited offer
- Ease of first action
- Free gift with purchase
- Quantity discount
- Attractive payment terms
- Speed of delivery
- Removal of fear of loss

6

MAXIMIZING
OPPORTUNITIES

You, like almost everyone else, are guaranteed to be leaving success behind with nearly every interaction. Whether from face-to-face appointments, telephone conversations, or marketing messages, you are bypassing huge potential for enhancing your sales success by leaving money on the table.

You may feel a little challenged by what you have just read and consider your conversion rates to be high, your customers happy, and business good. When growing a business, every moment counts, and regardless of your current level of success, the objective is always to reach a little higher and maximize your opportunities. Too many people enter a sales opportunity with the mindset that there are just two potential outcomes: success or failure. Instead of seeing things so black and white, color the shades of gray by building a number of successes in each interaction, raising the typical bar, and challenging yourself to see just how much you can get from every moment.

What this means is that you need to plan your levels of success before each opportunity and consider what there really is on offer. You might have an appointment with someone who has shown an interest in one particular product or service. Open your mind and think: what else could this person provide you with?

Things to consider:

- **Additional sales**—The easiest time to sell something else to someone is immediately after they've made the first buying decision.
- **Further appointments**—Increasing the frequency of the transaction is a fantastic way to grow a business, and planning the next appointment keeps you in control of this.
- **Referrals**—Asking for referrals should be part of your daily routine.
- **Cost savings**—If you also spend with this customer, they may be able to improve their offer to you. If you don't ask, then you certainly don't get.
- **A cheeky request**—Many of your customers will have a database of customers and send them regular newsletters. If you ask to be included in this, they may well agree.

Again, if you don't ask, then you don't get!

There is always more available to you. By considering the size of the opportunity before being within it, you are likely to achieve more from it.

This chapter explores some of the ways that you can get more from your moments and build on your successes.

STOP OVERSELLING

In modern business, your reputation is everything, and repeat transactions, follow-on sales, and referrals are vital to growing organically. When selling yourself, your product, or your service, it can be easy to become a little overzealous in your promises because of you desire to look good in the moment or make it easier to win the sale on the day.

Leave room in your sale to overdeliver with your results, and never, ever sell something for more than what it is. Making false promises can result in you sounding too good to be true and your value not matching the price you have presented. If it does not add up, the result is that the consumer loses trust in your ability to meet your commitments.

When things sound "too good to be true," the internal question asked becomes, "What's the catch?" To resolve this issue and win people around to your way of thinking, there are some simple solutions:

1. **Tell them the catch**—With every transaction, there is some bad news to go with all the good news. If you share the bad news also, it helps people see your offer for exactly what it is.

2. **Be proud of your price**—Not being proud of your price suggests that you don't believe it offers value. The more confident you are in your price, the more the consumer believes it is a fair price to pay.

3. **Set their expectation levels realistically**—Work off a minimum level of expectation and then go out and overachieve for your clients. By taking this approach, not

only will you win more business but you'll also maintain your customers for longer periods and create a referable reputation by exceeding expectations.

PRICING

The first lesson on pricing was served to me as a fourteen-year-old businessman, and the simplicity in this lesson has been reiterated in numerous offers, with dozens of clients, and still is something I need to continually remind myself of in my own business.

As a child I built a wildly successful car valeting business that started by asking for just £3 to hand-wash a vehicle. I soon realized I could charge £3.50 without any detriment to the decision-making process and was often given £4 for my efforts. The next natural move was to try £4.50, and this magically resulted in an added convenience to customers, as they paid with crisp five-pound notes and said, "Keep the change." I was on a roll and stepped again to £5.50, but I was immediately faced with resistance. Customers would postpone their appointments, defer their cleaning, or cancel altogether. I learned that the ceiling price for the service offered was £5, and I found this by testing it.

I meet many business owners who tell me proudly how they convert 100 percent of their opportunities. The truth is that we should price some of our customers out of the marketplace, and until we do so, we have not yet found our optimum price point. Your price should be calculated by what your product or service is worth to your consumer, and not what it costs you. Providing you can provide it at a price they are prepared to pay and make a suitable profit, then you are in business.

Look at your current pricing and consider it from the point of view of a customer. What does it say? How would you interpret it and what would you think if it was presented to you?

As your knowledge and experience grow, so does your competence, and in turn your prices should follow suit. In every profession, experience brings rewards. By improving your sales skills, you will be able to better demonstrate your value to your customers and improve your remuneration accordingly.

Test your pricing and continually try new price points until you are certain that you have found an optimum point. You may then look to introduce a premium and a value offering to sit on either side of your core product or service. If a customer is happy paying $5,500, then would it make any difference if you asked for $5,650 or $5,685? Keep nudging until you hit the point of resistance, and know that every dollar you successfully add to your pricing is 100 percent profit, with no additional expense and no additional workload.

YOUR DOWNSELL

Shortly you will learn the principles associated with securing an additional sale or upsell from your customer. Often overlooked, though, is the ability to rescue an otherwise unsuccessful opportunity with the introduction of a downsell. Customer acquisition is the most difficult action of all areas of business growth, and it is, therefore, useful to look for ways of capitalizing on all those sales scenarios in which you don't get the primary result you are looking for.

When you're unsuccessful in securing your initial outcome, consider what you could introduce as an alternative. This may mean resorting to an "easy first yes" or perhaps even just a small part of the anticipated order.

What I do know is that part success is far more satisfying than complete failure. Having the agility to introduce smaller decisions if your first action fails will bring significant additional business to you and provide you with the chance to overdeliver and reach your initial objective over time.

In my business, there have been many discussions in which it has been impossible for a client to secure my services as a speaker or trainer in person. The downsell has been a bulk order of books or an online training course. This would have always been a long way off of the initial goal, yet it still secured a profitable sale and in many cases resulted in further work with the client.

By not having a predetermined downsell, you create many scenarios where both parties lose.

THE SIMPLE UPSELL

The mastery of introducing a valuable additional sale at the point of purchase can be taught by studying one of the most operationally efficient businesses in the land. The global franchise McDonald's has mastered the ability to grow the average size of an order by asking a very direct question to all customers ordering one of their meal deals. The invitation to "go large" or "supersize" teaches you much of what you need to know about successfully introducing an upsell:

1. **Timing**—There is a perfect moment to introduce a further sale to your customer, and it is after the point of decision and before the point of payment. This window provides a period in which you have so much to gain and almost no risk of loss.

2. **Upcharge**—A quick decision can be made by adding a complementary purchase or additional quantity that does not exceed 20 percent of the original agreed price. Greater than this requires additional consultation and could slow your momentum.

3. **Consequences of customer rejection**—Rejection caries no consequences, and there is neither reprimand from the employer to the employee nor challenge from the server to the customer. The server's job is to ask the question and not worry about the outcome.

4. **Frequency of ask**—The request is made every single time, without fail and in every location across the globe. Consistency is the key, and the compound effect of this repetitive question results in millions of dollars in incremental sales every single year.

Understanding the elegance of this example, you should ask yourself if these workers are more skilled or less skilled than you. If this can happen in a global fast food retailer, then I am confident that you can replicate this in your business and achieve significant incremental revenues. Follow the rules, ask the question, and approach with the following mindset:

Some will.

Some won't.

So what!

The customers of McDonald's would have never missed the extra fluid or the handful of extra French fries. Making the extras available is all additional profit, and it won't be missed unless you make it available and invite your customers to step up.

CREATING OFFERS

There are only three organic ways to build a business:

1. Gain more customers.
2. Increase the size of your sales.
3. Increase the frequency of transactions.

When you are out shopping as a consumer, you are continually viewing examples of how companies are looking to entice an action from you to achieve one of these outcomes. I am asking you to open your senses and learn from the examples that exist all around you. By creating appropriate offers around your products and services, you can significantly influence the quantity and quality of transactions and improve your selling success.

There are six different types of offers I want to bring your attention to, and each has a very different application in order to maximize its results. When you understand how to use offers in your business, it's amazing what you can do to trigger even more of the right kind of results.

MULTIBUY OFFERS

You see these offers littering point-of-sale cards on the shelves of stores across the globe. Three for two. Buy four, get one free. Buy two for $5. Each of these offers is designed with a very specific purpose. The primary purpose of a multibuy offer is to switch loyalty to a consumable good, and you'll often see it on items such as toiletries. The initial compelling offer could be enough to entice you away from your previous chosen brand, and the quantity you leave with creates a commitment that may shift you to the new product as your new brand of choice.

If the offer were a discount off a single item, then the opportunity to switch your loyalty would be significantly reduced. Instead, the multibuy offer encourages you to buy more of the product than you really need. You become familiar with using that product, so when you go back to the store next and you see no special offers across any of the products, the product that you purchased through the offer is now your habitual choice and you have switched allegiance.

Use multibuy offers to add quantity to consumable items and encourage increased loyalty, so that the buyer becomes more invested in you and your products or services.

DISCOUNTED OFFERS

Although many offers can be used for many reasons, the primary reasons to discount ahead of a negotiation are first to clear unwanted stock and second to provide a highly incentivized, incremental sale to a brand new client.

Clearing through old stock is essential in any business, and even within a service-based offering you have chances to make price-led incentives to work through old material. Many coaches, consultants, and trainers have developed materials for purchase over the years that are no longer part of their core offering. Bundling these together and offering them at a fraction of their original price can be a great way of securing revenue from otherwise redundant items.

The second use becomes more relevant when you are aware of the lifetime value of your customers and are prepared to forfeit margin in a first transaction with the belief that you can make it back in follow-up sales. These offers need to be heavily targeted for maximum effectiveness and combined with a preplanned sales process to then grow the account later.

CONDITIONAL OFFERS

A conditional offer is a way of creating a set of qualifying criteria customers must meet in order to access an additional benefit. Qualifications could include

- The size of a transaction
- Speed of action
- Provision of additional data
- Commitment to an alternative action

The condition becomes the objective you are looking to achieve. Examples are

- Spend over $100 and receive 20 percent off of your next transaction.
- Order today and receive this free gift.
- Complete our questionnaire and gain a month's free access to (insert product).
- Bring a friend and both receive an extra item.

Conditional offers can grow average transaction value, introduce new customers, increase loyalty, and drive future sales.

MEMBERSHIP

Maslow's hierarchy of needs highlights the human need for belonging. In a world craving consumers' attention, having customers that belong to you is a huge asset. Almost every service-based offering has the ability to develop a membership model and for a recurring fee provide a package or bundle of services. Spreading their payment over a period provides a reduced barrier to entry at the start of a relationship and often an increase in total spending over the lifetime of the customer.

Turning your infrequent service into a recurring monthly overhead allows you to become habitual in your customer's routines. Also, through spreading their investment over a scheduled payment plan, you could be allowing them to decide to choose you earlier. The easier you make that for people, the more you can grow your customer base and their loyalty to you.

If you have a consumable product, something you'd like people to buy more than once, consider how you might be able to encourage your customers to commit to a recurring transaction and keep them coming back without having to decide. They decide once to receive until they say stop. That's a membership offer.

GIFT WITH PURCHASE

The best examples of these offers always exist on the cosmetics counters of department stores during the holidays. You might find that a typical bottle of fragrance is priced at $52, and that might be for the 1.5-ounce bottle. Moving to the 3-ounce bottle raises the price to $75. Now that the spend is over $75, the buyer qualifies for an exclusive gift of a purse, makeup bag, or beach towel with a perceived value of $50-plus. The result is that, given the choice between the two bottles, the bigger bottle is the clear winner because of the perceived extra value and since average transaction values are significantly increased over this period.

Gifts are used to drive transaction value across many markets and at all levels of transaction. Learn from the examples you see in your local food delivery outlets and watch how their offers of gifts are all at very precise points that mean you need to order just one more item to meet the criteria for the gift. Our local Chinese delivery offers a free sample platter on orders over $35, and our typical order for two totals just over $33. The result is I almost always order an additional dish to access my "free" gift.

Loss Leaders

A loss leader is selling something for less than what it costs you, with the primary purpose of driving additional traffic. A major supermarket retailer in the United Kingdom delivered an aggressive campaign for the launch of a Harry Potter book. They priced the book at just £5, and this in-demand product, combined with a very low price, resulted in floods of people choosing to buy that product from that store.

Where did they position that loss-leading product? Right at the back of the store—driving traffic through their organization and steering buyers past a variety of other products and offers, using the loss leader to secure masses of incremental sales on the day. You see this same approach with limited supplies of ridiculously priced products for high-volume sale days like Black Friday and Cyber Monday.

Should You Give Discounts?

Buyers are trained to ask you for discounts. This certainty should have you prepared in advance with a response.

Consider a scenario in which you asked for a discount in your life, perhaps on a substantial purchase like a house or a car. When you achieved a reduction in price, I imagine you felt a sense of achievement and satisfaction … only later to question yourself, wondering whether an even better price was possible. In the same scenario, the seller is similarly questioning whether you would have paid more. The result is that both parties are not convinced they achieved the best deal.

When you buy something in a retail store, you accept the price is the price and go about your day without a second thought about that transaction. You are comfortable that you paid the same as anyone else would have paid on that day and feel content in your purchase. Do all that you can to protect the integrity of your pricing and provide consistency to all buyers.

The only time to consider altering your pricing is if what you are getting in exchange for the discount is something that equates to the reduction in fee. If you are being asked for a better price, then think: what can you take in return? Things to consider are as follows:

- Increased order size
- Long-term commitment from the customer
- Improved payment terms
- Introduction to another organization you can do business with
- Testimonials or case studies to support your future marketing

Question their request for a discount, listen to their answers, and instead of altering your price, look to see how you can enhance your value to them without reducing the price.

Ways you can consider enhancing value are as follows:

- Increased payment terms
- Giving extra instead of reducing the price
- If their budget does not stretch, then reducing the specifications

A Secret Ingredient to Success

Often overlooked and immensely valuable to your customers is the pure convenience attached to doing business with you. The easier you are to transact with, the more likely you are to secure the dozens of marginal opportunities that exist year after year.

Large companies like airlines and technology businesses that make things like ride-sharing apps polarize this with the pure convenience of doing business with them. A click of a button, the remembering of my details, and synchronization across multiple communication devices means that my ability to shop with any of their competitors is reduced to almost impossible.

You may not offer this same level of convenience, but you can easily increase the value you provide by thinking about what the buyer values most. What are the little things you can do that remove barriers to transactions? How can you join the dots on their behalf when things are complex? How available can you make yourself when things do not work out as planned?

I have worked with my current print supplier for years, and I have no interest in ever changing. I am continually presented with the opportunity to change supplier, and I am certain many of these options could provide more attractive pricing. The reason for my loyalty is that they make everything really easy for me. They take an order over the phone and provide a 70-day account, they then make minor amendments in-house to artwork files without rejecting them and without further expense, they take calls in the evenings and on weekends, and they have moved mountains to meet impossible deadlines and challenging logistical demands. The convenience factor that they provide makes them our default supplier and someone I regularly recommend. They are a partner to our businesses and get rewarded for the value that they bring. Take a look at your own processes and see how easy you make it for your customers. Simply by removing any barriers and being prepared to be flexible, you will win more business.

THE FOUR Rs

Succeeding in sales requires huge self-discipline, personal responsibility for growth, dogged determination, and resilience to setbacks. The quest for more, more, and more can quickly have you on the treadmill, working harder and harder without focus or awareness of the world around you.

Earlier in the book we talked about your high payoff activities, and one that was mentioned was the importance of planning and review. When people are given the choice of performing well, doing better, or doing their best, the consensus is always to try your best. My personal belief is that this approach can self-sabotage your potential, because the likelihood that you actually did try your best is minimal. By focusing on "better" as opposed to "best," you can discover the components to improve that will have you on a journey of continual self-improvement.

To activate this process, I regularly set aside time to properly plan and review my actions through a process I call my Four Rs. I encourage you to do the same.

PART 1—REFLECTION

Take a moment to do a thing that is relaxing for you. Sit in your favorite spot, go for a walk or a run, or take a long shower or bath and consider just how far you have already come. Look backward to the start of this period and reflect on all that you have achieved. Stay present in the moment and don't look to the future at all—be kind to yourself and enjoy reliving the experiences that have helped you along so far.

PART 2—REVIEW

Once you're relaxed, it's time to sit down and work on the work you have already done. Work through the appointments and actions you have recently completed, and list the specific things that went well. Stay away from any criticism, and exhaust every component of practical positivity from your previous actions. It may help to write out physical lists and keep focused until you have exhausted everything that you succeeded at and would like to keep as part of your protocol.

PART 3—REFINE

Now is the time for you to look for improvements, only instead of cataloging the things that you did wrong, look through the lens of what you would do differently if faced with the same opportunities again. This is your time to be true to yourself and look at the improvements you can make and the opportunities you left behind. Identifying these as actions for "next time" is a kinder and more productive process than beating yourself up about failing to achieve.

PART 4—RESCHEDULE

Following every activity or action, there should always be a next step. Your previous activities can all be repeated and should be scheduled in periodically. Many of the prospects and customers you have created need to be contacted again, and your list of improvements for next time should all be applied to specific and tangible events. Choosing to take action and apply the lessons you have just discovered keeps you sharp and continuing to improve. Scheduling the tasks to specific actions, calls, and meetings keeps you in control, protects your memory, and frees your anxiety to focus on growth.

7

OVERCOMING INDECISION

A large focus of selling is to move people from the position of "no" and secure a positive outcome. My personal experience tells me something different. I believe that the bigger opportunity for sales success lies within influencing the volume of people who are stuck in the position of "maybe" or looking to decide at another time.

Following a sales conversation, you are certain to find many people remain undecided after all your efforts. They may provide you with an objection, excuse, or reason why they can't do business at this time. In all the industries I have served and all the people I have trained, the objections received typically fall into one of the following categories:

- Not the right time
- Need to discuss with someone else
- Shopping around

- Happy with existing supplier
- Need some time to think about it
- Too expensive

This chapter will explore how you can avoid, overcome, and negotiate this indecision to result in increased sales from the opportunities you create.

AVOIDING OBJECTIONS

Pretty much every objection that you have ever faced could have been avoided if you'd asked great questions earlier on in the sales process. Take a look at your most common objections and think about how they can be avoided before you even recommend your solution. If the objections you receive are recurring, then your first step should be to develop a series of questions that you can ask during the qualification stage that allow you to gather the evidence required to avoid the objection altogether.

Perhaps the best example of this is something from my experience of working with sales teams in the furniture industry. When selling furniture, we faced several objections, and many were related to two of the key profit drivers within the business. First was the requirement to have couches sealed with a treatment that prevented staining following spills. Second was the sale of an upholstered footstool to complement a couch.

The most common objections received for these two products were as follows:

- We are very careful and never eat and drink on our furniture.
- We have no room for a footstool.

Examine these two objections, and you quickly realize that they are more likely to be excuses than facts, although they're also very difficult to challenge without calling the buyer a liar (even though we know they don't always tell the truth). Understanding this, I set to work developing a series of questions to be used earlier in the conversation, prior to either of these options being introduced, that delivered answers that made it nearly impossible for consumers to share these typical excuses. We developed questions such as, "Apart from yourself, who will be using the furniture?" and would then follow with, "And a spot of entertaining?" After listing the initial users, everybody would admit to entertaining. I guess nobody admits to having no friends?

I could then ask, "Is it going in your best room or your everyday room?" The answer to this question either confirmed extensive use or that it needed to remain looking like new. The follow up was then, "How long have you had your last couch for?" Regardless of the answer, the next question was always, "I guess you are looking for this to last the same time or longer?" To which the answer was always a resounding yes.

This gave evidence for recommending the fabric protection, but we still had the space issue for the footstool. We would come straight for it with the question, "So, how big is the room?" Regardless of the answer, our reassuring response would be, "Wow, that is a fair-sized room." It would then not be uncommon for them to draw out the proposed layout and create space as the diagram appeared. Throughout their sketching, I would ask questions about their entertaining—how they provided seating for extra guests and what they did for storage—all building evidence to support the later recommendation of the footstool.

Gathering this collective evidence perfectly positioned the recommendations of the additional products toward their reasons and not mine. I could say, "Because of the fact that you said XYZ, we recommend ABC," as a framework for introducing fabric protection, footstools, or any other additional item using the knowledge gained in the earlier conversation.

This process almost doubled conversion rates, and its principles have been introduced to businesses across the globe to spectacular positive effect.

Instead of embellishing the option of "yes," you are better off using questions to destroy the option of "no." Qualify the true opportunity and only recommend the right thing to the right people and for their right reasons.

Selling is earning the right to make a recommendation, and your time invested in earning that right always ensures your recommendations are received with more authority and authenticity.

TACKLING OBJECTIONS

Every objection really should be treated as a disagreement, and you should take personal responsibility for the fact that they have raised an objection, since it may mean that they have grabbed the wrong end of the stick. Throughout the years, I have developed a simple system that acts as a framework to overcome every objection presented to you.

1. **Clarify the objection**—Remember that success in sales is all about maintaining control of the process. The second they raise an objection, they are challenging that control and can easily switch it. Think about an interview scenario: it's

the person asking the questions who is in complete control. Knowing this, if we treat every objection as a question and look to regain control by asking a further question, we get closer to the real objection. Ideal questions involve simply getting them to explain their objection further. A universal example, and my default response, is: "What makes you say that?"

2. **Agree and apologize**—Given that an objection is viewed as a disagreement, you can easily deflate it and find some level ground by agreeing with them and then apologizing. Once you have done this, you have a platform to respond from and won't fight fire with fire. If someone objects because they feel your price is expensive, you could say, "I agree entirely. When I am looking to buy things, I look for the best possible value too, and I am really sorry, because I clearly have not explained myself right."

3. **Check if it is the only concern**—Ask if this is the only factor stopping them from moving forward. If they agree, you have only one objection to overcome. Missing this step can result in a game of tennis in which they continually present further objections as each is overcome.

4. **Receive it positively**—Take the fact that they have objected as proof that they are interested in what you do, and not that they are not interested. It will have a very positive impact on your posture.

5. **Answer positively**—It is very easy to focus on what you cannot do when somebody presents you with an objection. Simply focus on what you can do instead. If the objection is based on price, then simply explain what you can do for their budget instead.

6. **Summary close**—After explaining what you can do, the safest closing tool when dealing with indecision is to close in summary form. Simply break the decision into between five and ten small decisions and ask direct, yes-focused questions, knowing that when they say yes to each question, they then agree to the whole thing.

NEGOTIATE LIKE A PRO

Business is simple but not easy. The difference between average and great is typically the last 10 percent of the process, and it can quite often be the time when most people give up. The ability to negotiate effectively when you do not get your own way will make a significant contribution to your success and be infinitely more rewarding. To maneuver these tricky conversations, follow these nine simple principles to help you become a master negotiator and ensure that people come round to your way of thinking more often:

1. **Arguments end with losers**—Nobody wants to be a loser. The challenge with arguing in a sales environment is that if you are the winner, then your prospect is the loser. Avoid arguments at all costs.

2. **Show respect for the other person's opinions**—Now, you don't have to agree with them, but they are entitled to their opinion. Understand their reasons for their point of view and try to understand.

3. **Admit when you are wrong**—Admitting to what you don't know or have got wrong will add weight to anything that you do know.

4. **Encourage the easy yes**—To bring prospects around to your point of view, ask multiple simple questions that lead to yes answers. By answering yes to those questions, your prospect will find it easier to continue saying yes.

5. **Talk less**—The biggest reason for a misunderstanding or failure to communicate effectively is not listening.

6. **Let the other person believe that it is their idea**—Introduce your ideas as questions and not statements. That way, your prospect can choose your point of view as their own.

7. **Try honestly to see things from the other person's point of view**—This may seem hard, but it is vital to show empathy when negotiating. Putting yourself in their shoes will help you understand why they think what they think. This angle will add substance to your side of the negotiation.

8. **Dramatize your ideas**—Whether you're selling a product, service, or idea, enthusiasm always helps to convince. Simply by becoming more charismatic when presenting your viewpoint, you will make it far easier for people to agree with your line of thinking.

9. **Throw down a challenge**—Always finish your negotiations with a challenge or ultimatum. A good example would be "So, if I can get this done today, are we okay to confirm the order now?"

Expert negotiation comes with practice. To practice, at first be brave enough to enter negotiations without expectations of the outcome and without fear of loss. Do not give in too easily, and believe in yourself. Typically, it is a mix of skill and confidence that wins a negotiation.

Persistence

At the start of the book you were encouraged to think about your perfect or ideal customers. These perfect opportunities, and even the less-than-perfect ones who have ignored you, rejected you, or made promises to act and failed to follow through, all still have a value to you and your business. It can be easy to take this lack of success in sales very personally and feel bruised by your failure, as well as to interpret this rejection as a forever decision and to never revisit it.

As a consumer yourself, you are aware that your circumstances are changing all the time, and the same is true for your customers. What is considered "the wrong time" for your potential customer today could easily become the right time tomorrow through a variety of internal or external factors. Understanding this, it is your responsibility to never forget a prospect and do all that you can to remain in their minds for when the opportunity may arise.

Keep a list of all your NNTs (No Not Todays) and continue to stay in touch, ensuring you are the first person they think of when their circumstances change. This includes communicating with them in the following ways:

- Regular e-mails or newsletters
- Adding them to your social networks
- Dropping in to say hello
- Picking up the phone

Without being overbearing, the objective is to have them know that you are still thinking of them.

Let's focus on the point of just picking up the phone. A good friend and early mentor of mine tells a great story of persistence and how it helped land the largest training contract he had ever secured, which has supported him and his family with a fabulous lifestyle. He called his dream customer every week at the same time for eighteen months and continually got no further than the personal assistant. However, not put off from achieving his goal, he continued to call, and after building great rapport with the assistant, he finally got put through to the owner and won his appointment. This resulted in a contract that revolutionized his business. Without question it was well worth the effort. My advice is to never, ever, ever, ever give up!

PLAYING DEVIL'S ADVOCATE

You will regularly find times where you receive a conceptual interest in your product or service and fail to get it to something specific that you can invite them to buy.

During my time in the property business, we developed a fantastic long-term investment product in which the model involved owning a freehold property in the sun that you could use personally. It forecasted a 1,000 percent return over a 15-year period and would then continue to deliver an income. The concept and the opportunity was interesting to almost everybody I met, and requests for more information were overwhelming. E-mails were sent, meetings arranged, and brochures dispatched, and all with minimal return.

Something needed to change. The true challenge was getting enough potential customers to the point that they were looking at a specific property in a specific development at a specific price. Without this, I had no control and the whole thing remained up in the air.

Searching for inspiration, I reached into my memory to look for times when decision making was easy and remembered the times my brothers, my sister, and I had sat as children and entered into the land of make believe with my mother's catalogues. We could readily make decisions about the items we would love to purchase for our imaginary homes. This peculiar logic led me to develop a closing technique that I have since named the "Devil's Advocate" close.

Each time a level of interest was established from a potential customer, I created a hypothetical scenario by using the preface "Let's just play devil's advocate for a second...." What followed would be a series of questions that resulted in the deductions required to identify whether, if they were to invest in a property, the one they would choose would be this one. Getting to this point allowed many further real-world conversations, gave me the ability to present real information, and regularly turned conceptual interest into actual purchases.

Could hypothetical questioning deliver you the information you need to progress more sales?

8

PROTECTING YOUR INVESTMENT

Growing your customer base, increasing your orders, and winning business from your competition is only part of the job. Developing a community of customers who continue to spend with you, refer you to others, and build your reputation is the long-term goal, and taking a long-term view means following the correct maintenance plan for all you have invested in.

View your customers, ambassadors, and prospects like an ATM that, when cared for correctly, will print you money as and when you need it. Protect your investment by serving your community with the right tools and showing them that you care about them. Focusing solely on new customers leaves you vulnerable and stifles long-term growth as you start losing customers as quickly as you created them. Returning to the theme of relationships and dating, your customers need continual attention and must feel like you care about them, so stay connected with regular touch points. Group your contacts in order of priority and develop a care plan for each group that is maintainable and consistent with the purpose of keeping your customers engaged.

Large businesses can employ big teams to work on account management and retention of their customer base. The modern world means that communication channels are plentiful, and even with limited resources you can stay visible in the hearts and minds of your customers, providing you use the right tools for the right jobs.

Although not an exhaustive list, this chapter focuses on the account management tools I identify for my clients as being essential in building and managing your community of contacts and continually reminding them to shop with you. Many of these tools are evolving and changing all the time and your options here are abundant. Remember that this is a book on selling skills and not a marketing guide, to explore the full potential of these communication channels then you may wish to explore further resources by other professionals. But please look at the principles behind each channel mentioned and how they can help you to increase your sales success.

THE DATABASE

Without question, a good database is the hub of all great account management processes. A database should include all relevant contact details for all customers, suppliers, and potential customers. It should show their past value to you financially and also include their expected future value. You should then keep an up-to-date biography on each person in your database, allowing others to understand your relationship, and it should store any useful facts. Attached to each record, you should keep a running timeline of contact and correspondence, allowing you to always have great information to recall. In addition, the ability to forward plan and set reminders prevents you from needing a perfect memory.

Years ago, systems that provided this service were a significant investment, and small businesses relied on spreadsheets, diaries, and client files. Technological advances mean that you can access software that provides a framework to do all of this at no further expense to yourself. Simply enter the phrase "business CRM system" into your search engine, and you will be impressed by the incredible choices.

THE DROP-IN

Spending time in person with your most valuable contacts provides an effective way to remind your customers to shop with you. This can be achieved by showing your face in person when you are local. Sometimes unannounced, perhaps arranged at short notice, or even a scheduled meeting—every time you meet with a potential customer, you have the potential to influence a sale. When you meet with an existing client, you will have the opportunity to further cement your relationship and uncover new areas where you can help each other; when you meet with a contact, you have the chance to share their contacts for further business development opportunities. Plan your future meeting points with customers and prospects and decide your minimum expectations for each contact. A giant reason that people leave their suppliers is from not feeling valued. Face to face time is a great way of showing that you care. You can also use your future travel plans as a guide to stay in touch with others and reach out on the occasions you find yourself in their locality.

THE PHONE CALL

We have already established that picking up the phone is a catalyst for making stuff happen. Please don't forget your existing customers, and schedule regular calls to discuss their progress and future plans. This is your chance to check their happiness with the work completed to date, as well as gain insight into their plans and what you can do to assist. Regular calls can be both unannounced and scheduled. With your key relationships, committing to a regularly scheduled contact provides a promise that keeps you in the conversation and has them see you as an important part of their team. Think of the times you are travelling and how your time could be easily wasted. Prepare a call list that would allow you to turn low pay off periods of time into high pay off sales activities by reaching out to your customer base and creating further opportunities.

THE NEWSLETTER

Sending a regular hard-copy newsletter to your existing customers can be a fantastic way of keeping them engaged with your business and ensuring that you are kept in mind and is likely to have a far greater deliverability rate than its electronic counterpart. The question of how often you write a newsletter will continue to go unanswered. My take is that its frequency should be consistent and you should write as often as you have something worth saying. Being paper based, it should be simple to read and full of images. Consider that it will be read as a break from the daily routine, so it should be light entertainment. Physical mailings are becoming fewer and fewer, so delivering something of value in this form to your customer can be a way to share information and stand out.

THE E-NEWSLETTER

The biggest difference between your electronic newsletter and its paper-based rival is that only the minority of people you send it to will actually open it, let alone read it. Be diligent in your consistency and send it at the same moment for each period so that your contacts expect to receive it. Deliver value to them and provide only information that they may find useful. Inboxes are cluttered with poor-quality e-mail communications, so to cut through the noise, you need something that earns its place. Your e-newsletter is your "catchers mitt" for all of your contacts and is the one piece that can reach everyone you have ever connected with and has given their permission to stay in touch with you.

Treat it with that level of respect and only commit to produce something you can commit to and are proud of.

THE BLOG

This is a fantastic tool for positioning yourself as an expert within your industry. Ideally attached to your website, it's where you can regularly post your thoughts, ideas, and opinions on matters that will be of interest to those you communicate with. Having a blog gives you a voice to share great information, can make you more findable by your target market, and is sharable with your existing customers. Linking to your articles within your newsletters drives traffic back to your site.

For content on your blog a great place to start is to consider the most common questions you are asked in your industry and construct well written pieces that deliver answers to these questions. These pieces can then be shared by you and others when this need arises and act as a resource to your efficiency and add credibility to your advice to future and existing customers.

THE FACEBOOK PRESENCE

Facebook is currently the largest online community in the world and has the attention of the majority of English-speaking consumers in most marketplaces.

A page can be a tool for credibility and to communicate with your fans, and a Facebook group is a useful way of staying connected with customers who are part of the same experience. Personal profiles should remain exactly that—personal. Encourage your contacts to connect with your page, post varied content that appeals to them, and build support groups for your core offering to leverage your time.

One of the largest frustrations I face with platforms like Facebook is the ever changing landscape to the strategies that work. Understand that what works today may not work so well tomorrow and that this is always the case. Create a minimum performance standard for posting and engagement, you can then experiment with their paid advertising options and other strategies to grow your reach and be more specific with your targets and messaging. As you experiment then be sure to test what is working and only invest your energy and resources into those that are delivering you results.

THE TWITTER ACCOUNT

Imagine Twitter as the busiest-ever train station in rush hour. Conversations are happening everywhere, and you are not sure what to say or who to listen to, but no doubt there will be a few interesting conversations going on.

I find Twitter far more useful for listening to others and joining conversations, rather than looking for something profound to say myself. Follow all of your key customers and pay attention to what they are posting. Retweet their posts and join in their discussions if you want them to notice you.

Educating customers on the use of the # symbol when grouping information can allow them to communicate in groups effectively and easily. We will use #exactlyhowtosell to monitor conversations about this book, so please search it on Twitter and see what you find.

THE LINKEDIN ACCOUNT

Connecting with all your existing customers on LinkedIn can give you huge benefits. First, you can learn so much more about them from their detailed personal profiles, but also you have gained a further way of directly contacting them. LinkedIn e-mails often generate a higher open rate than standard bulk e-mails and can get you noticed more effectively. A further benefit is that if your contact ever moves on, you are connecting to them as an individual and not via the business. That way it will be easy to contact them again once they reach their new role.

A further tool within LinkedIn is the ability to create groups. By creating a group for your customers, you again have a further method of communication and can create a community for them around your area of expertise and add huge value as the leader within that space.

THE WEBSITE

Your website is a fantastic tool for managing your existing customers. Every time you bring people to your website, you have the chance to introduce additional products and services to them. If you provide resources to your customers, then make them available from your website and introduce additional offers and products to them on their journey to reach the resource they are looking for. Your social media and e-mail campaigns can all drive traffic back to your site, and well-positioned offers will bring results. By adding content for complimentary product and service offering to your site you can direct your existing customers back to the site with your other campaigns and soon introduce them to other ways in which you can help them, hence growing the value of your existing customers.

THE GET-TOGETHER

The big corporations know the value of getting their best customers together for high-level hospitality scenarios. Getting your customers together and demonstrating how you value them is a proven method of increasing their loyalty. Use new product launches, seasonal events, celebrations, and office moves all as excuses to get your customers together. Add additional levels of success to your events by giving VIP invites to existing customers and inviting them to bring along friends who could soon grow into future customers. Document these events with video and photos, share them in your digital media, and encourage attendees to do the same to maximize your return on investment.

THE LETTER

Keeping things simple, let's just focus on the letters you already send your customers—perhaps statements, reminders, or even invoices. Each of these letters provides a sales opportunity, and every form of outbound communication can carry an additional message as well a primary purpose. Consider the extra value you can get from every mailing by adding a small message or including a secondary communication. Every communication provides a commercial sales opportunity, and it is down to you to realize them.

THE E-MAIL OFFER

Unlike an e-newsletter, this piece is designed to trigger a response or action from the reader. E-mail campaigns continue to be remarkably effective, providing you adhere to some simple rules:

- You have permission to send, and the recipient has opted in to receive promotional e-mails from you.
- Your offers are targeted and relevant to the recipient and not generic in their approach.

Once you've targeted the right customers, you have a number of barriers to overcome.

BARRIER NUMBER 1: GETTING YOUR OFFER OPENED

Just getting an e-mail opened can be challenging. It relies on a compelling subject line and a trusted sender address. Just as with newspapers, the better the headline, the better the uptake. Your subject line should be designed with the purpose of getting the e-mail opened, rather than labeling the content of the e-mail.

The best emotion to trigger to ensure successful open rates is intrigue or curiosity. If you make the recipient curious as to the content of the e-mail, they become more invested in opening it. Monitor the subject lines that land in your inbox and draw influence from those that pique your interest.

BARRIER NUMBER 2: GETTING YOUR OFFER READ

Once your e-mail is opened, the reader will make a reflex decision whether to read it. Your opening sentence must capture the reader's interest and encourage them to read more. Subheadlines can help to lead people through the copy and make reading it more simple.

BARRIER NUMBER 3: GETTING THEM TO TAKE ACTION

If your offer gets read, it is paramount that the call to action is clear, prominent, and repeated. It should be as simple as possible for your reader to take action and painted out in clear simple steps. Confusion at this stage will result in no action taken and no sale. By repeating your action two or three times throughout your offer, you can significantly increase your click-through rates. A further area in which you can reiterate your call to action is in a postscript.

THE DIRECT MAIL OFFER

Although direct mail is delivering diminishing returns for many industries, I believe that as long as houses are built with mailboxes, a direct mail offer has a place in your communication track. As digital marketing dominates, a direct response mailer can be a refreshing alternative. Execution is the key to success, and personalization, creativity, and authenticity deliver the goods here.

Building on the success of handwritten cards, I often work with clients to produce low-volume, targeted direct mail campaigns that are highly personal. In a recent test, we measured the inbound inquiry level from a very simple split-test direct mailing. We produced a printed event invitation to be sent to just 100 of the client's existing customers. Fifty were sent on their own with a generic covering letter and resulted in not one inquiry. For the other 50 we wrote a very short personal message on a Post-it note and adhered it to each flyer before sending. This resulted in an inquiry rate of eight from 50 invitations.

Consider how you can build low-volume, highly targeted and personal direct mail campaigns and create huge impact on the right people to drive powerful actions from your existing customers.

THE GIFT

Corporate gifts have been around for years, and the gift market is a huge industry. Yet still I see mistake after mistake as, with the best intentions, companies provide gifts that are of little value to their customers and in turn provide little return on investment. Diaries, calendars, mousepads, mobile phone holders, cheap pens, and stress balls are all examples of gifts I have received that have all passed over my desk without a second thought.

Think of the gifts that will increase your value to your customers and be of genuine value to them. Be personal and consider their hobbies, lifestyles, and interests.

Something that has worked fantastically for me is the gifting of great books that I have read. When I have read something that I believe will be of value to someone in my network it is quite frequent that I will purchase a copy for them and send it off with my compliments.

Objective of every gift is to SHOW that you care and be of genuine value to the recipient.

THE PAT ON THE BACK

All business leaders and decision makers love recognition. Whether it's a simple thank you or some lavish praise, providing it is delivered with sincerity, it is a great way of adding value for your customers. Saying thank you is a minimum, but there are many ways you can step this up with a little extra attention. Perhaps a client of yours receives an industry award, is recognized in the press, or goes through a significant life event. Use these moments to reach out and acknowledge their achievements. Send cards, press cuttings, and tokens of appreciation as a means of letting them know that you too are celebrating their successes.

Track your clients personal and professional communications and pro-actively look for opportunities to recognize their successes.

CERTIFICATES AND AWARDS

How can you certify your customers for their work with you? Whether it is a product guarantee, a recognition of their loyalty, or attendance at a training session or an event, anything you can do to add their name to a piece of paper containing your logo with the potential of it being framed or displayed reinforces the value your client gets from you.

Placing something of this nature in their possession also provides significant opportunity that this item will be displayed and create a reminder to them of the value you provide and also a potential talking point to bring you into more conversations when you are not even there.

THE TEXT MESSAGE

This is the only method of communication that is almost certainly both opened and read. The world can stop for a text message, as people stop midconversation to check their phones. The text message should be used as a timely reminder for simple actions. One of the best uses I see is when fast food delivery retailers send their latest offers by text to previous customers on Friday afternoons. Consider how a text could remind someone of an expiring offer, introduce an event invite, or simply recognize an important event in their world.

THEY ALL TUNE IN TO THE SAME STATION

In every communication with a customer, it is important that you understand that they really only tune into one frequency. The station they are listening to is called Wii FM, which stands for "What's in it for me?" With every statement you make, you must put yourself in the customer's shoes and ask yourself, "So what?" In doing so, you will ensure that all your communication is benefit led and has the recipient's interests in mind.

IT IS THE THOUGHT THAT COUNTS

When you take a retrospective look at your life and reflect on the recognition, praise, and rewards showered upon you, I am certain you are able to count on one hand the number of occasions you remember vividly and that have really left their mark.

As a final thought, I want you to consider acknowledging those of value to you and your business. In today's fast-paced society, taking time to recognize effort above and beyond the call of duty will give your business the edge and make you leap out from the crowd. Whether you wish to reward excellence in your team, show gratitude to a valued customer, celebrate success with a partner, or show recognition to a prospect, success in sales is an amplification of the relationships you build. Genuine care will always be in vogue.

Financial reward can be an incentive but is rarely the best option and over time could cost a fortune. You've heard it said that "It's the thought that counts," and in business this gives you a massive chance to shine. Rain genuine praise on your employees when they achieve, say thank you to your customers at every given opportunity, let your partners know their efforts are appreciated, and do all you can to go the extra mile.

When saying thank you, be sure to use the right tool for the job. With e-mail overload and the whole world going mobile, a successful way of getting noticed is to go back to basics. Sending a handwritten card or letter in acknowledgment of achievements or just to say thank you will win you respect and appreciation. I believe it is possible to build a business by sending cards to customers and prospects, since there are so many opportunities to say thank you or acknowledge special occasions. The sincerity of the message is all-important. It should be personal and heartfelt—don't use the occasion to send marketing literature. Take the time to write neatly by hand.

If you want different results and to be seen as different from your competitors, then start behaving differently.

ABOUT THE AUTHOR

Phil M Jones has made it his life's work to demystify the sales process, reframe what it is to "sell," and help his audiences to learn new skills that empower confidence, overcome fears, and instantaneously impact bottom line results. The author of five best-selling books, and having been awarded as the youngest-ever winner of the coveted "British Excellence in Sales and Marketing" award, Phil is currently one of the most in-demand assets from companies worldwide.

He's by no means your typical sales expert. Phil's famous for his powerful "Magic Words" and his highly engaging, practical approach to what is often a subject that is littered with hype and power-hungry "gurus."

His vast knowledge and experience can be simplified into just three areas:

1. Acquiring more customers

2. Having them come back more often

3. Helping them spend more when they shop

With the experience of over 2,000 presentations in over 50 countries across five continents, Phil has a busy and active travel schedule. When not on the road, you will find him at home in New York City or in his peaceful retreat in Buckinghamshire, England.

To find out more about the author, please visit: www.philm jones.com.

Acknowledgments

Writing a book is hard. These things do not happen by themselves and are not achieved by the work of one person. Getting to the point of scribing this part of the prose can typically fill me with dread, as I worry profusely about the people I have forgotten to mention.

This time is very different, as I am 100 percent certain that I will be forgetting thousands of individuals as the collation of the ideas, thoughts, and experience packed into this book has been made possible by the dozens of mentors that have served my career, the hundreds of talented people I have worked with, and the millions of people I have had the privilege to call customers.

It's the customers who remain the greatest asset of any business, and these are the people who teach us and have guided so much of my career to date. If I have ever had the privilege of serving you, then I thank you. The lessons served by the marketplace have taught me more than any book could ever have shared with me, and I am humbled by the knowledge that understanding business means understanding people, and that means getting close enough to learn from them.

I must never forget to thank the hundreds of mistakes that I have made already and the ones I am yet to make. For it is the lessons served by these mistakes that provide me the real life contrast to have confidence in the principles shared in this book.

Specifically there are a few very special people who possibly have no idea on the impact they have had on my life . . . .

My first mentor, "Chalky" White, who was the first teacher to tell me that maybe I am the one who knows what is best for me and gave me the confidence to carve my own path.

Norman Smith, for giving me a chance as a kid and allowing me to think bigger and act bigger in the workplace, long before my years should have allowed.

Carl Menard, Peter Lee, and Dave Payling, for believing in me long before my time and teaching me the foundations on which to build and manage a big business.

Adam Jobson, for being the one person who has never doubted me and trusting me with a part of his future.

Mum and Dad, for giving me the education to be curious, the humility to fail, and the courage to keep moving forward. I will be eternally grateful to the rope you let out on me and the safety net you have kept secured and always made available.

For the book itself, which has been a whirlwind, and from concept through to creation would not have happened without the foresight and entrepreneurial spirit demonstrated by Shannon Vargo and Kelly Martin at John Wiley & Sons, who helped me realize that this builder's son from a small town in England may actually be an author.

Trena White, Gabrielle Narted, and the entire team at Page Two strategies for being my true friends in the publishing world and always delivering with professionalism and grace, and helping me navigate the landscape of the publishing world.

Meeting the deadline of a book creates an anxiety-fueled pandemonium. I am submitting a manuscript archived in eternity and anchored to my reputation. This means that it needs to be legible for people other than me to read it, and the herculean editing effort delivered by Jenny Govier has been inspiring.

Finishing this book resulted in a 72-hour period of my life locked for 16-hour days in our cabin in Buckinghamshire, and if it weren't for my beautiful and talented wife Charlotte, there is no way I would be here today. Seeing her put up with my obnoxious grumpiness as I worked to get this finished reminds me how lucky I am to have found the perfect woman who still loves me at my worst!

My final thank you is one that is dedicated to possibly the most important person of all. You. Your taking the time to actually read my structured ramblings is the reason I went through the pain of crafting this piece, and reading every word of a book is the greatest gift you can ever share with an author. Thank you for allowing me to play a part in your story, and please share your comments with me personally and allow me to know how your story unfolds.

Index